6476

DATE DUE

Metro Litho
Oak Forest, IL. 60452

AMERICA the BEAUTIFUL
MISSOURI

By William R. Sanford and Carl R. Green

Consultants

Warren R. Solomon, Ph.D., Curriculum Consultant for Social Studies, Department of Elementary and Secondary Education, Jefferson City

Duane Meyer, Ph.D., President Emeritus and Professor of History, Southwest Missouri State University, Springfield

Lawrence O. Christensen, Ph.D., Professor and Chairman, Department of History and Political Science, University of Missouri-Rolla

Mary K. Dains, Assistant Director, State Historical Society of Missouri; Associate Editor, *Missouri Historical Review*

Robert L. Hillerich, Ph.D., Bowling Green State University, Bowling Green, Ohio

CHILDRENS PRESS®
CHICAGO

Quilts such as these are among the handcrafted items made by Missouri artisans.

Project Editor: Joan Downing
Associate Editor: Shari Joffe
Design Director: Margrit Fiddle
Typesetting: Graphic Connections, Inc.
Engraving: Liberty Photoengraving

  2 3 4 5 6 7 8 9 10 R 99 98 97 96 95 94 93 92 91 90

Library of Congress Cataloging-in-Publication Data

Sanford, William R. (William Reynolds), 1927-
  America the beautiful. Missouri / by William R.
Sanford and Carl R. Green
    p.   cm.
  Includes index.
  Summary: Introduces the geography, history,
government, economy, industry, culture, historic
sites, and famous people of the "Show Me" state.
  ISBN 0-516-00471-9
  1. Missouri—Juvenile literature. [1. Missouri.]
I. Green, Carl R. II. Title.
F466.3.S26 1989   89-35082
977.8—dc20   CIP
                                                   AC

Union Station, a St. Louis landmark and once the world's busiest train station, has been converted to a marketplace that includes shops, restaurants, and a hotel. Great Hall (above), the station's waiting room, has been beautifully restored.

TABLE OF CONTENTS

Chapter 1
THE VIEW FROM
THE GATEWAY ARCH

THE VIEW FROM THE GATEWAY ARCH

In England, the ancient arches of Stonehenge have stood during centuries of British history. Imagine for a moment that the soaring Gateway Arch at St. Louis has done the same. What occurred at this site beside the Mississippi River?

Early Indians hunted and fished near the great river. Then came the Spanish soldiers of fortune. The Spanish were followed by French explorers, who glided down the Mississippi in their canoes. The pace picked up in 1764 when Pierre Laclède founded a town called St. Louis on the banks of the Mississippi. Forty years later, Lewis and Clark set off from a camp near St. Louis on their trek to the Pacific Ocean.

The first half of the 1800s saw the migrations that would give the Gateway Arch its name more than a century later. Pioneers on their way to the unsettled territories of the West crossed the Mississippi River at the frontier town of St. Louis—the gateway to the West—to reach the starting points of the trails that led to their destinations.

In the mid-1850s, Samuel Clemens—better known now as Mark Twain—piloted steamboats on the river between St. Louis and New Orleans. Then, in 1904, came the excitement of the St. Louis World's Fair. In 1945, residents of St. Louis were filled with a deep sense of pride when Missouri's favorite son, Harry Truman, became president of the United States.

In truth, the arch was not completed until 1965. But even though it has not stood during most of Missouri's colorful past, it stands now as a symbol of the central role the Show Me State has played in American life.

Chapter 2
THE LAND

THE LAND

During the late 1700s and well into the 1800s, thousands of land-hungry Americans from the East moved westward. Weary families stopped at St. Louis, the gateway to the West, to rest before beginning the long trek that lay ahead of them. While they waited for new caravans to form, many settlers looked around and decided they'd gone far enough. Rich farmland, a moderate climate, and navigable rivers made Missouri look like a bit of heaven on earth.

Missouri's 69,697 square miles (180,515 square kilometers) make it larger than thirty-one other states. Indeed, the state is larger than all of the six New England states put together. Missouri's eight neighbors are Iowa on the north; Illinois, Kentucky, and Tennessee on the east; Arkansas on the south; and Oklahoma, Kansas, and Nebraska on the west.

OCEANS AND GLACIERS LEAVE THEIR MARK ON THE LAND

Long before the first human beings set foot on Missouri's black soil, nature was shaping the land to its own design. Missouri's story goes back hundreds of millions of years.

Over five million years ago, the Gulf of Mexico covered much of the southern United States. Ocean waters reached as far north as the junction of the Mississippi and Ohio rivers. Over tens of thousands of years, the land rose, then sank, then rose again. When the water receded for the last time, Missouri had become a part of a broad, nearly flat, plain.

With the dawn of a new ice age about a million years ago, shorter, cooler summers couldn't melt the thick blankets of snow that winter left on the ground. The snow turned to ice, and in the far north, the ice sheets grew thicker and heavier. Finally, the weight became so great that the sheets began to move. They had become glaciers. The rivers of ice spread southward, eventually reaching Missouri, where they stopped at the Missouri River. The last ice age reached this line about twenty thousand years ago. When the weather turned warmer, the ice began its long retreat.

The glaciers helped to make northern Missouri one of the most fertile farming areas on earth. Along with rocks and gravel, the glaciers carried tons of fine silt with them. When they melted, they left immensely fertile soil behind. Prairie grasses sprouted and anchored the black earth so that it couldn't blow away.

Over time, the forces of nature thus marked Missouri with distinct geographic features. Geographers divide Missouri into four major regions: the Glaciated Plains, the Osage Plains, the Ozark Highlands, and the Alluvial Plain.

The land north of the Missouri River is the Glaciated Plains region. Much of the land is covered with fertile soil left by the glaciers when they retreated. Over the years, wind and rain have combined to erode the plains into a region of low, rolling hills.

The Osage Plains, sometimes known as the Western Plains, are the low, rolling prairies of western Missouri. The region is sandwiched between the Missouri and Osage rivers, and was never touched by the glaciers.

The Ozark Highlands, located in the south-central part of Missouri, is the largest geographic region of the state. Swift

Prairie grass at Cuivre River State Park, in the Glaciated Plains region

streams have cut through the Ozark's forested hills to create valleys where the bluffs rise as much as 500 feet (152 meters) above the streambeds. The soil is thin and rocky, but the region's lakes, caves, and mountain scenery make it a favorite recreational area.

The small Alluvial Plain region is sometimes known as the Bootheel because it sticks out of the state's southern border like the heel of a cowboy boot. The Alluvial Plain was built up by the Mississippi River, which left thick layers of mud and sand behind when it flooded. The rich soil is perfect for growing cotton, rice, and soybeans.

Vilander Bluff, on the Meramec River in the Missouri Ozarks

THE OZARKS

The green and lovely Ozark region is one of Missouri's most
important geographic landmarks. The Ozark Highlands is the
only large area of high ground between the Appalachians and the
Rocky Mountains. The region's 55,000 square miles (142,450
square kilometers) are bounded by five rivers—the Mississippi,
Missouri, Osage, Neosho, and Arkansas. The wooded hills mark
the western limits of the forests that once covered the eastern
United States. When early settlers left the Ozarks, they knew that
dusty, treeless prairies lay ahead.

Meritt Rock Cave, on the Current River, is one of the more than five thousand caves that have been discovered in Missouri.

The charm of the Ozarks begins with the fact that nature's earth-building forces lifted all of the hills to roughly the same height. The state's tallest peak, Taum Sauk in the St. Francois Mountains, rises in the Ozarks 1,772 feet (540 meters) above sea level. Spring-fed streams and rain-swollen rivers have cut deep, curving valleys between the peaks. When some of the springs ran dry, they left caves and sinkholes behind. More than five thousand caves have been found in Missouri, of which twenty-four are open to visitors. Aboveground, forests of oak, hickory, and pine trees grow on steep hillsides, creating a world of great beauty. Where human beings haven't intruded, this world is alive with birds, deer, fish, and wildflowers. To protect the unspoiled wild rivers, the government has set aside the Buffalo Natural River and the Ozark National Scenic Riverways.

In the forests that cover about one-fourth of Missouri, trees such as oak, hickory, ash, cottonwood, and maple are common.

The Ozarks abound in natural wonders. Northern trees, such as river birches and beech, grow in the cool valleys. Lichen that are more often seen in the Arctic can be found clinging to north-facing cliffs. Desert scorpions make themselves at home among sunbaked rocks. The white-tailed deer and black bears, once hunted nearly to extinction, have been saved by strict conservation laws.

For all their wild beauty, the Ozarks are not a wilderness. Hikers and boaters are seldom more than 10 miles (16 kilometers) from a road. Small, hidden towns nestle in the green hills, waiting to welcome visitors. The damage done by heavy logging and careless burning has been repaired over the past fifty years. Today, some 2.5 million acres (1 million hectares) have been set aside as national forests.

The Great Riverboat Race on the Missouri River is an annual event.

RIVERS, LAKES, AND STREAMS

Much more than most states, Missouri's geography is dominated by its rivers. The state claims two of the world's greatest rivers, as well as many smaller rivers and more than eleven hundred streams. Missouri's major rivers are the Missouri (the Big Muddy) and the Mississippi (Father of Waters). The Show Me State's folklore is full of tales about the Missouri and the tons of silt it used to carry. There was a time when farmers liked to say, "The Big Muddy's too thick to drink and too thin to plow!" Old-timers claim that the river "separated the men from the boys." The boys, they said, became boatmen on the Mississippi; the men went up the Missouri.

In spring, the volume of water flowing down the Missouri can reach 800,000 cubic feet (22,654 cubic meters) a second. More often, the river is shallow and filled with sandbars. Steamboats that plied the Missouri were designed with flat-bottomed hulls so they could carry heavy cargoes in water only a few feet deep. One writer declared that any boat that could not "climb a steep riverbank, go across a cornfield, and corner a river that is trying to get away, has little excuse for trying to navigate on the Missouri."

In the old days, the Missouri often cut new channels when it flooded. Riverside towns have been swept away by the rampaging river, and boats have been picked up and dropped miles away. Today, dams and flood-control systems have greatly reduced channel cutting and the amount of silt carried by the Missouri.

After the Missouri joins the Mississippi, the two rivers seem to run side by side. By the time the Mississippi flows the 200 miles (322 kilometers) to its meeting with the Ohio River, however, the waters are fully blended. For much of its length, the Mississippi has been lined with flood-control levees. These earthen banks average 15 to 25 feet (4.6 to 7.6 meters) in height, but the river often breaks through. In 1937, the Mississippi rose 56 feet (17 meters) and flooded large areas of southern Missouri. In 1988, by contrast, a drought left the river so low that boat traffic came to a standstill.

Missouri's other major rivers include the St. Francis, the Osage, the Black, the White, the Grand, and the Chariton. Just as important as the rivers are the state's abundant underground water resources. Wells drilled in the Ozarks often yield up to 600 gallons (2,271 liters) a minute. Big Spring, near Van Buren, is one of the nation's largest single-outlet springs. Fed by groundwater, Big Spring produces a maximum daily flow of 846 million gallons (3,202 million liters).

Although Missouri has no large natural lakes, its artificially made lakes are another important resource. The Harry S. Truman

Reservoir is the largest artificially created lake in the state. Lake of the Ozarks, created when Bagnell Dam was built on the Osage River in 1931, is the state's second-largest lake. Other important lakes include Taneycomo, Clearwater, Table Rock, and Wappapello. These lakes, with their fishing, water sports, and natural beauty, attract visitors from all over the world.

A CHANGEABLE CLIMATE

Missourians have a ready reply for visitors who complain about the weather. "Be patient," they say, "it will change any minute now." In truth, Missouri's weather does vary greatly. A day that dawns warm and sunny over southeastern Missouri may turn windy and cold on the northwest prairies.

In general, winters are cold without being frigid. January temperatures range from 25 degrees Fahrenheit (minus 4 degrees Celsius) in the northwest to 34 degrees Fahrenheit (1 degree Celsius) in the Bootheel. Summers are long, warm, and humid. Temperatures in the summer average about 80 degrees Fahrenheit (27 degrees Celsius) across the state. In July, the temperature often climbs from 66 degrees Fahrenheit (19 degrees Celsius) at sunrise to 90 degrees Fahrenheit (32 degrees Celsius) at midday. Clinton, in west-central Missouri, recorded the state's highest temperature in 1936—118 degrees Fahrenheit (48 degrees Celsius). In 1905, the temperature in nearby Warsaw dropped to a record low of minus 40 degrees Fahrenheit (minus 40 degrees Celsius).

Nature is kind to Missouri when it comes to rain and snow. The northwest receives an average of 36 inches (91 centimeters) of precipitation each year. Winters are fairly dry, and almost half of the rain falls during the May-to-August growing season. The southeast receives an average of 47 inches (119 centimeters), most

Missouri's summers are long, warm, and humid, and its winters are fairly dry, with an average snowfall throughout the state of about 20 inches (51 centimeters).

of which comes in spring and autumn. Across the state, snowfall averages about 20 inches (51 centimeters) a year. As might be expected, northern Missouri receives more snow than does the south.

Although Missourians say their climate is "temperate," the weather can swing from one extreme to another. As 1988 proved, the rains fail on an average of once every ten years. The resulting droughts cause great damage to crops and livestock. As if to offset the droughts, some years bring heavy rains and flooding to one or more parts of the state. Summer thunderstorms also generate whirling tornadoes whose 250-mile- (402-kilometer-) per-hour winds can destroy entire towns.

Chapter 3
THE PEOPLE

THE PEOPLE

In a state populated by many different kinds of people, is there such a thing as a "Missouri way of thinking"? Many Missourians would answer that question with a loud "Yes!" They like to remind visitors that they are from the Show Me State. That nickname dates back to a day in 1899, when Missouri Congressman Willard Vandiver grew weary of hearing another lawmaker praise his own state. Vandiver responded, "I come from a country that raises corn, cotton, cockleburs, and Democrats. I'm from Missouri and you have to show me."

To Missourians, this means that they look at the world with a healthy skepticism. If they like an idea after examining it from all sides, they'll think about adopting it as their own.

WHO ARE THE MISSOURIANS?

Though about 98 percent of Missourians were born in the United States, they trace their heritage to many cultures and races. In Missouri, people of different cultures came together to form a single government and a diversified economy.

The majority of today's Missourians are descended from English, Scotch-Irish, German, and Italian ancestors. Some are descendants of immigrants from France, Czechoslovakia, Poland, Switzerland, Belgium, or China. Newer additions to the state's ethnic mosaic have come from Mexico, Central America, the Soviet Union, and Southeast Asia.

St. Louis, with a population of 453,085, is the largest city in the state.

About 10 percent of Missouri's population is black. Many are descendants of African slaves, some of whom were brought to the region as early as 1720 to work in the lead mines opened by the French.

POPULATION AND POPULATION DISTRIBUTION

According to the 1980 census, Missouri's population of 4,916,759 ranks fifteenth among the states. In the 1980s, the state's rate of growth was only half that of the national average. The Census Bureau predicts that the population will grow by no more than one-tenth of 1 percent by the year 2000.

As recently as the 1930s, Missourians were evenly divided between rural and metropolitan areas. Today, three out of four Missourians live in metropolitan areas, the largest of which are St. Louis, Kansas City, Springfield, Joplin, Columbia, and St. Joseph. Within these metropolitan areas, however, people have been moving out of the central cities and into the suburbs. In the

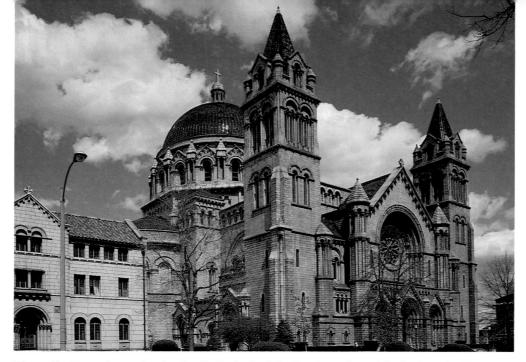
The collection of mosaics in the Cathedral of St. Louis ranks with the best in Europe.

ten-year period between 1970 and 1980, for example, the city of
St. Louis lost more than 25 percent of its population.

RELIGION

Most Missourians are Protestants who belong to Baptist or
Methodist churches. Other major Protestant denominations in the
state include Assembly of God, Episcopal, Presbyterian, and
Lutheran. About one-third of the population is Roman Catholic.
The Jewish religion, with congregations centered mainly in the
cities, has flourished in the state since the late 1830s.

A SAVING SENSE OF HUMOR

Life hasn't always been easy in Missouri, and the people have
had to develop a saving sense of humor. Many Missourians enjoy
tall tales, and most of all they admire anyone who smiles in the
face of danger. That explains why Missourians delight in telling

stories like the one about the riverboat captain. Seeing that a passenger was worried by the dangers of steamboat travel, the captain drawled, ''Ma'am, I've been on the river for thirty years. In all that time, I ain't yet met a man who said he drowned in the Missouri.''

Missourians also tend to favor the underdog. Perhaps that's the reason some people admired the James brothers back in the 1800s. The James boys were no-good outlaws and murderers who held up banks and trains. Robbing trains was fine with plenty of folks who resented the power of the railroad barons.

Only a Missourian could have twitted the umpires the way Hall of Fame baseball player Casey Stengel once did. Just as the plate umpire was about to throw him out of a game, Casey lifted his hat . . . and let a bird fly out.

A RECORD OF ACCOMPLISHMENT

Missourians like to laugh, but they don't laugh at success. Missouri has produced successful people in many fields. Scientist and educator George Washington Carver has been a role model for people of every race. Anyone who shops in a J. C. Penney store is sharing in the retailing genius of another Missourian. People who remember birthdays and holidays with a Hallmark card can thank Joyce Hall, whose company in Kansas City became a great American success story. People as varied as Nobel Prizewinning poet T. S. Eliot and Dizzy Dean, one of baseball's all-time great pitchers, were born in Missouri.

The list of Missouri's scientists, entertainers, athletes, writers, inventors, and politicians is almost endless. There's no doubt about it—the citizens of the Show Me State have played a leading role in the development of the nation.

Chapter 4
THE BEGINNING

THE BEGINNING

When much of the world's water was locked up in the glaciers, the oceans fell, exposing a land bridge between Asia and North America. Bands of Asiatic nomads followed game animals across this bridge about twenty thousand years ago. The search for better living conditions led the new Americans southward. About ten thousand years ago, some of them reached the Missouri area.

THE FIRST MISSOURIANS

These first Missourians were hunters and gatherers who made simple tools and weapons from stone. Their carefully tended campfires provided warmth and light and were used to harden the tips of their spears. They cooked stew by dropping hot stones into tightly woven baskets filled with water. They made clothing and moccasins from animal skins.

The first people who made permanent settlements in Missouri were another hunting and gathering culture—the Bluff Shelter People. They lived in shallow caves on the edge of steep hillsides. Over thousands of years, these early people improved their way of life. They learned to fish and to plant and harvest crops. They made axes, needles, awls, and fishhooks from wood, stone, and bone. They invented pottery and made birchbark canoes for travel along the region's many rivers. About two thousand years ago, the Bluff Shelter People became part of a more advanced civilization.

Among the relics left by Missouri's Mound Builders are a shell amulet (left) and a Bird Man tablet (right) from the Mississippi Culture.

THE MOUND BUILDERS

Between 2000 B.C. and A.D. 1500, the people of the Midwest developed a highly complex culture. Food was plentiful, and the population increased rapidly. People lived in stockaded towns and buried their dead in mounds of varying shapes. Skillful hands created beautiful artworks of shell and bones. Tribes joined in a loose confederation that stretched from western New York to Nebraska and from Wisconsin to the Gulf of Mexico.

The first mounds, built by people of the Hopewell Culture, were simple, rounded heaps of earth. As mound building developed, the sites became larger. Some of the later mounds were built in the form of giant birds and serpents.

In Missouri, many of the mounds were built on the edge of bluffs that overlooked the Mississippi and Missouri rivers. The people who built the mounds lived nearby in small villages protected by wooden stockades. Their thatched-roof houses were small, but the mounds were not. The mound near Caruthersville, in southern Missouri, is 400 feet (122 meters) long, 250 feet (76 meters) wide, and 35 feet (11 meters) high.

The Hopewells gradually gave way to the Mississippians. By A.D. 1200, the Mississippians had built the most advanced culture north of Mexico. Their ceremonial center was located on the banks of the Mississippi at a place called Cahokia, in present-day Illinois. The huge temple complex was located on the east bank, but the site spread to the west bank as well. Today, the cities of East St. Louis, Illinois, and St. Louis, Missouri, occupy that same land.

At Cahokia, flat-topped pyramids served as temples. From evidence found inside the mounds, it is clear that the Mississippians traded over a wide area. Their trading territory reached from the Rocky Mountains to the Atlantic coast. Archaeologists believe that the similarities between this culture and that of Mexico's Mayans and Toltecs prove that there was regular contact between the two regions.

For reasons that are not clearly understood, the mound-building culture collapsed. When the Europeans first arrived in the 1500s, the mounds were overgrown with grass and trees. In time, some mounds were opened to reveal human bones, weapons, and jewelry.

THE OSAGE

The French explorers of the 1690s found three Indian tribes living in Missouri—the Missouri, the Iowa, and the Osage. Although all three lived on land once occupied by the Mound Builders, they followed simpler, more nomadic lives.

The Missouri and Iowa were branches of the powerful Sioux. Neither group ever numbered more than a thousand men, women, and children.

The Osage were the largest and most important of the Indian groups living in Missouri. In the late 1600s, the Osage occupied a territory that extended from the Arkansas River in the south to the Missouri River in the north. The Osage were noted for their

The Osage and the Missouri were two of the three Indian tribes living in Missouri when French explorers arrived. During his travels among the Indians of the Midwest, George Catlin captured the likenesses of Clermont, chief of the Osage (left), and Haw-che-ke-sug-ga ("He Who Kills Osages") (above), chief of the Missouri.

height. Many were over 6 feet (1.8 meters) tall, and a few of the men topped 7 feet (2.1 meters).

Many of the Osage lived on the prairies beyond what is now Missouri's western border. Others made their homes in the western Missouri woodlands and along the rivers. The Osage traveled on foot or by dugout canoe. They built their permanent villages on carefully chosen high ground. The sites were always near water and game and were always easy to defend. Within each village, several families occupied each large lodge. The sturdy lodges were built of poles covered with woven mats or bison hides. Many Osage settlements were located north of the Ozarks along the Osage River. From there, the Osage carried on a busy trade in bison hides and fox, beaver, and wolf furs.

The traditional Osage way of life centered around hunting and warfare. In summer, hunting parties traveled to the prairies to stalk bison. Winter weather sent the hunters into the southern hills after deer and bear. The Osage grew pumpkins, squash, corn, and beans and gathered wild fruit, berries, and nuts. Whenever war erupted, the men streaked their bodies with red and black paint.

THE FIRST EUROPEANS

Gold! Indian gold beyond imagination! In the early 1500s, Hernando Cortés and a handful of soldiers conquered Mexico and carried off the golden treasure of the Aztecs. Francisco Pizarro led an expedition to Peru and took the gold of the Incas back to Spain. Were there more riches to be found? Tales of golden cities just over the horizon led Spanish explorers northward.

Hernando De Soto landed in Florida in 1539. By May of 1541, his party had crossed the Mississippi River. Some historians believe that De Soto traveled as far north as Missouri, where he rested his weary soldiers before turning south. Although he didn't find gold, De Soto was probably the first European to sight the mighty Mississippi.

At about the same time, Francisco Vásquez de Coronado was leading an expedition north from Mexico. Coronado found Indian pueblos and great herds of buffalo, but he didn't find any gold. In the summer of 1541, Coronado and his men camped in what may have been western Missouri. Along the way, some of their horses escaped, and the Indians stole others. These few horses, plus those lost by other expeditions, gave birth to the wild herds that changed the Indian way of life.

FRENCH EXPLORERS REACH MISSOURI

By the early 1600s, the French were well established in Canada. The rich fur trade lured explorers and trappers farther and farther south. When they finally reached the Mississippi River, the French were overjoyed. They believed the great river would lead them westward to the Pacific Ocean.

In 1673, Father Jacques Marquette and Louis Jolliet led a small party down the Mississippi. Traveling in two canoes, the Frenchmen became the first Europeans to see the mouth of the Missouri River. Marquette and Jolliet didn't turn back until they reached the Arkansas River. By then, they had realized that the Mississippi led to the Gulf of Mexico, not to the Gulf of California.

René-Robert Cavelier, Sieur de La Salle, followed in Marquette's footsteps. The ambitious La Salle wanted to found a French empire that would stretch from Canada to the lower Mississippi Valley. In early 1682, La Salle led an expedition down the Mississippi. When he reached the river's mouth, La Salle claimed the "country of Louisiana" in the name of his king, Louis XIV. Louisiana included all the land drained by the Mississippi River and its tributaries—from the Ohio Valley to the Rocky Mountains, and as far south as the Gulf of Mexico.

MISSIONS, MINES, AND SETTLEMENTS

France's empire in the New World now stretched from the St. Lawrence River in the north to New Orleans in the south. To

Pierre Laclède (left) and René Auguste Chouteau (right) built a trading post on the west bank of the Mississippi River in 1764 that later grew to be the city of St. Louis.

make up for a shortage of settlers, the French sent small bands of Catholic priests to build missions. Each mission was expected to convert the Indians, provide a fur-trading station, and hold the land for France. The first mission in Missouri was St. Francis Xavier, founded in 1700 near modern-day St. Louis. Before the mission was abandoned three years later, French traders had explored and named much of Missouri's geography.

In the early 1700s, Missouri became the center of a frenzied search for silver. It started in 1714, when Antoine de la Mothe Cadillac was attracted by rumors of rich silver deposits. Cadillac, who was governor of the entire Louisiana region and founder of Detroit, found deposits of lead, but no silver. Back in France, Sieur de Lochon, who had explored the area, was loudly declaring that Missouri's hills were bursting with silver ore. The French people rushed to invest their money in a company that promised to mine the silver. In 1720, Philip Renault led a group of French miners and black slaves to Missouri to carry out the plan. Like Cadillac, he found only lead. The scheme collapsed, leaving the investors with nothing but their worthless stock.

Renault didn't give up. For the next twenty-four years, he mined the plentiful lead ore. After the ore was smelted in crude furnaces, it was poured into molds shaped like horse collars. The "collars" were fitted to pack horses for transport to Fort Chartres in Illinois. Later, Renault switched to two-wheeled carts and laid out Missouri's first crude road.

STE. GENEVIEVE AND ST. LOUIS

With the lead mines producing well, the French built their first permanent settlement in Missouri about 1750. Ste. Genevieve was located on a Mississippi River crossing, near some salt springs. The town had been built too close to the river, however, and spring floods began to carve away the riverbank on which Ste. Genevieve was located. Between 1781 and 1794, the townspeople were forced to move their buildings to higher ground a few miles to the north. By then, Missouri was no longer in French hands.

Through a secret treaty with Spain in 1762, France gave up the land in Louisiana west of the Mississippi River. In 1763, the French lost Canada to the British in the treaty that ended the French and Indian War. Thus, the land west of the Mississippi went to Spain, and the territory east of the river fell into British hands. The French governor moved to St. Louis, where he remained until Spanish officials arrived in 1770.

St. Louis, then six years old, gained prominence as the crossroad for the British and Spanish empires in North America. The city had been founded in 1764, when fur trader Pierre Laclède and his stepson, René Auguste Chouteau, built a trading post on the west bank of the Mississippi, just below the mouth of the Missouri. The first settlers were French Creole families from across the river in Illinois.

After Americans led by George Rogers Clark (in doorway) captured the British fort at Kaskaskia, Illinois, in 1778, the British and their Indian allies raided St. Louis.

SPANISH MISSOURI HAS A NEW NEIGHBOR

The Revolutionary War brought dramatic changes to the Mississippi Valley. In 1778, Americans led by George Rogers Clark captured the British fort at Kaskaskia, Illinois. The Spanish officials in St. Louis offered to help recapture the fort if the British and their Indian allies would counterattack. Instead, a force of British traders and a thousand Indians raided St. Louis. Captain Fernando de Leyba, with only fifty soldiers, organized the town's defenses and drove off the attackers.

At the end of the Revolutionary War, the territory between the Appalachian Mountains and the Mississippi River became part of the United States. Almost overnight, American settlers began moving into Illinois. The Spanish feared that if the upstart Americans settled in Missouri, they would be hard to control. In order to preserve Spanish rule, they offered tax-free land grants to both French and American settlers. In return, the new owners were expected to become Spanish citizens.

The promise of land grants was a strong lure. Colonel George Morgan of Philadelphia founded a colony at New Madrid, near the point where the Ohio joins the Mississippi. Within a few years, a thousand Americans were living in Missouri. Among the new settlers were Daniel Boone and Moses Austin. Boone, the nation's most famous woodsman, was an old man by this time. Austin, better known for his part in colonizing Texas, set up a successful lead mine west of Ste. Genevieve in 1798.

MISSOURI BECOMES AMERICAN

As the new century began, Napoleon Bonaparte's conquest of Spain returned the Louisiana Territory to French hands. Almost at once, the French closed the port of New Orleans to American shipping. The loss of a port on the Gulf of Mexico was a serious blow to western farmers, miners, and trappers. The problem was solved with the Louisiana Purchase in 1803, when Napoleon sold the Louisiana Territory to the United States for $15 million. On March 9, 1804, Captain Amos Stoddard of the United States Army took possession of Missouri and raised the Stars and Stripes.

THE LEWIS AND CLARK EXPEDITION

With the Louisiana Purchase, the United States owned a huge western territory, but little was known about it. In 1803, President Thomas Jefferson sent explorers Meriwether Lewis and William Clark to map the Missouri River, study the region's resources, and open a route to the Pacific Ocean. In May 1804, starting from St. Louis, the two men led an expedition upriver.

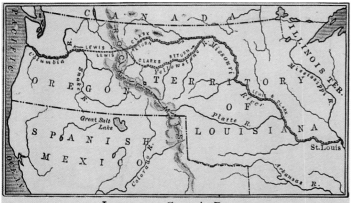

LEWIS AND CLARK'S ROUTE

The Lewis and Clark expedition left St. Louis on the way to the Pacific Ocean in May 1804 and returned in September 1806. During the trip, William Clark kept a diary and made sketches of the wildlife encountered by the party (right).

Forty-seven days later, the expedition reached the "Kanzas River," near what is now Kansas City. Clark kept a careful diary and made sketches of the land's natural features.

Despite the blazing heat, Lewis and Clark made good progress. They celebrated the Fourth of July near the present-day city of St. Joseph and wintered in North Dakota. In the spring, guided by an Indian woman named Sacajawea, Lewis and Clark pushed on through the mountains. The party finally reached the Pacific in November 1805, and returned to St. Louis in September 1806.

Jefferson read the expedition's report and realized that Missouri was the key to opening the West. He rewarded Lewis by making him territorial governor. Clark, who was admired and trusted by the Indians, served as governor from 1813 to 1821. Neither man was popular with the settlers, who felt they were too quick to take the side of the Indians.

RELATIONS WITH THE INDIANS

In the early 1800s, President Jefferson wanted the United States to remain neutral in the European wars between Great Britain and France. In Missouri and on the northwest frontier, the settlers saw the world differently. They believed that British traders were encouraging the Indians to attack them. Relations with the land's original inhabitants, never easy, now became inflamed.

By 1800, the original Missouri tribe had been so weakened by disease and tribal wars that it no longer existed. Other tribes had moved to Missouri, however, after being uprooted from their lands in the East.

When the United States went to war with Britain in 1812, the Sac, Fox, Osage, Delaware, and Shawnee pledged to remain loyal. These pledges did not keep other tribes from raiding American settlements, however.

After the war, many of the tribes met with Governor Clark at Portage des Sioux. The Indians signed peace treaties that bound them to move farther west, to Kansas and beyond. By 1820, there were only six thousand Osage, Sac, Fox, and Shawnee Indians scattered across Missouri. Even so, the settlers complained that the Indians were "wasting" good farmland.

Meanwhile, land-hungry Missourians were eyeing the rich Indian lands along the Platte River. At first, President Andrew Jackson defended the Indians, but he finally gave in to political pressure.

The treaty that was broken had promised the Indians that they could keep their lands "forever"—but forever lasted for only six years. The Iowa, Sac, and Fox received $7,500 for land that was worth thousands of times more. The last Indian tribe in Missouri, the Osage, gave up their land in 1825.

Chapter 5
THE PIONEER ERA

THE PIONEER ERA

The Louisiana Purchase had opened the way for the first great wave of new settlers. They spread across Missouri, from the fertile river valleys to the green hills of the Ozarks. Most flooded in from the nearby states of Illinois, Kentucky, and Tennessee, but families also came from North Carolina and Virginia.

FRONTIER LIFE

The majority of the new settlers were of English or Scotch-Irish descent. Many moved into the Ozarks, where they carved farms out of the wilderness. These new Missourians built log cabins, carved their own furniture, and wove their own cloth. Clever hands made banjos and fiddles so that dancers could enjoy the lively jigs and reels that were the ancestors of today's country-and-western music. Life on the frontier bred qualities such as independence, self-reliance, a stern morality, and respect for the land.

With land to clear and crops to cultivate, children didn't spend much time in school. In at least one district, however, the settlers hired a traveling teacher each winter to bring some "book learning" to the community. One visitor remembered the young Missourians this way: "They begin to assert their independence as soon as they can walk, and by the time they reach the age of fourteen, have completely learned the use of the rifle, the arts of trapping beaver and otter, killing the bear, deer, and buffalo, and dressing skins and making . . . leather clothes."

New settlers were encouraged to come to Missouri and were welcomed by those who had come before them.

With land cheap and plentiful, new settlers were welcomed by their new neighbors. Entire families would gather to help the newcomers get started. With the help of skilled and willing hands, a log cabin could take shape between sunrise and sunset. After the work was done, it was time for a hoedown. Someone would strike up a lively tune on a fiddle, and a square-dance caller would shout out the steps. Clapping and laughing, the dancers could forget for a moment that life on the frontier was a hard struggle for survival.

STATEHOOD AND THE WESTERN MOVEMENT

By 1812, Missouri had developed enough to become an independent territory with its own elected legislature. Missourians elected a house of representatives, but the governor was appointed by the president. The right to vote was limited to white adult males who had lived in the territory for at least a year.

An artist's version of St. Louis as it looked in 1854

In 1818, Missouri applied for statehood. The request touched off a bitter debate. If Missouri joined the Union as a slave state, it would upset the balance in Congress between free states and slave states. The argument was resolved by the Compromise of 1820. Maine would be admitted as a free state, and Missouri as a slave state. The rest of the Louisiana Territory was divided, with slavery outlawed north of 36 degrees and 30 minutes north latitude. On August 10, 1821, Congress admitted Missouri as the Union's twenty-fourth state.

During those years, trade and commerce were picking up. In 1819, the first steamboat paddled slowly up the Missouri River. The *Independence* carried a cargo of flour, whiskey, sugar, and iron castings to Franklin. Later that same year, a second steamboat, the *Western Engineer*, steamed upriver to the junction of the Missouri and Kansas rivers. Trails led deep into the Rocky Mountains where a breed of independent fur trappers known as "mountain men" lived far from civilization. Each year, Jim Bridger, Jedediah Smith, and the other mountain men left the Rockies to trade their furs for the next year's supplies.

As the population grew, towns sprang up along the rivers and on the trade routes. In 1822, a wagon route called the Santa Fe Trail was opened to carry trade goods between Independence, Missouri, and Santa Fe, New Mexico, which was then a province of Mexico. Prairie schooners carried woolens, tools, and mirrors to exchange for silver, mules, furs, and horses. Not all of the new towns survived. In 1828, the bustling town of Franklin slid into the Missouri River during a flood.

Western Missouri was also the starting point of the 2,000-mile (3,219-kilometer) Oregon Trail. Trappers, explorers, and settlers headed for the trailheads at Independence, Liberty, and St. Joseph. The crowded streets of these dusty frontier towns were lined with hotels, saloons, and the shops of wagonmakers and outfitters. Steamboats arrived almost daily to unload new settlers and the tons of equipment and supplies they needed for their trek west. Gold was found in California in 1848, and in 1849, the flow of settlers heading west turned into a flood of "Forty-Niners."

THE MORMONS

A darker chapter in Missouri's history was written during these same years. Mormon Joseph Smith, the leader of the Church of Jesus Christ of Latter-day Saints, chose Independence as a place of refuge for his followers. By 1832, more than a thousand Mormons had settled in the area. The local people feared that the industrious Mormons, who usually voted in a bloc, would gain control of local politics. Violence broke out, and the Mormons were forced to move to Caldwell County. Even though the state legislature had given them the right to settle there, new conflicts soon arose. After several bloody incidents, Smith moved his people to Nauvoo, Illinois, in 1839.

EUROPEAN IMMIGRATION

The first wave of European immigrants arrived after Missouri became a state in 1821. In the mid-1840s, repeated failure of the potato crop drove hundreds of thousands of people out of Ireland. Of the Irish who came to Missouri, some found jobs building the railroads, and others hired out as day laborers in the rapidly growing towns and cities. Many of the Irish immigrants settled in St. Louis, Buchanan, and Jackson counties.

Late in the 1840s, a new surge of immigration reached the state. Large numbers of Germans, already unhappy with the lack of freedom at home, had received glowing reports of Missouri's opportunities. When they arrived, most of them settled in communities around St. Louis and in central Missouri.

Each year seemed to bring new faces and accents to Missouri. In the decades after the Civil War, thousands of Italians joined the tide of immigrants. They settled in Kansas City, St. Louis, and in many smaller towns.

THE CIVIL WAR ERA

A Missouri slave named Dred Scott was the plaintiff in a famous lawsuit concerning the spread of slavery. In 1857, the United States Supreme Court angered the North by turning down Scott's plea that he should be a free man. Scott based his case on

Dred Scott was a Missouri slave who was denied his freedom in a famous case that was tried before the United States Supreme Court.

the fact that he had lived in the free territories of Illinois and Wisconsin. The Court also declared that efforts by Congress to limit the spread of slavery were unconstitutional.

When the Civil War started in 1861, only one Missourian in eleven was a slave. Even so, the state was divided by the question of slavery. When President Lincoln called for troops to defend the Union, Governor Claiborne Jackson refused. Jackson controlled the state militia, but Union supporters formed Home Guard units. In St. Louis, the Home Guards were given guns from the federal arsenal. Under the command of General Nathaniel Lyon, they marched to Jefferson City and captured the state capital. Jackson fled, and the antislavery forces quickly formed a pro-Union government.

As a result of these maneuvers, Union troops were in control of Missouri by 1862. A Union victory at Pea Ridge, Arkansas, choked off the South's last major attempt to recapture the state. The fighting didn't stop completely, however. Pro-Union raiders from Kansas attacked western Missouri towns where people favored the Confederacy. Southerners retaliated by organizing guerrilla units.

The war was long and bitter. More than a thousand Civil War battles were fought on Missouri's soil. Of the 150,000 Missourians who put on uniforms, more than two-thirds served in the northern armies. Civilians paid a high price, too. Raids by guerrilla irregulars from both sides burned fields and houses and killed many people. Altogether, 27,000 Missourians were killed during the war.

RECONSTRUCTION

Thanks to strong antislavery feelings and the quick action of the state militia, Missouri had stayed in the Union. In January 1865, Missouri became the first slave state to free its slaves.

But Missouri was a border state—and a slave state—whose loyalties during the war had been divided. Some members of the Republican party, known as Radicals, were determined to punish the South—including border states such as Missouri. In Missouri's General Assembly, Charles D. Drake, the leading Radical, led the fight to adopt a new state constitution. The resulting constitution of 1865 required public officeholders, the clergy, and members of many professions to swear an ''Ironclad Oath'' that they had

Union General Nathaniel Lyon, who had captured the Missouri state capital for the Union in June 1861, was killed two months later in the Battle of Wilson Creek.

never been disloyal to the Union. Clearly, former Confederates could not swear such an oath, and they were removed from office.

Over the next ten years, former Union General Francis P. Blair led the battle to end Radical rule. Blair united a scattering of regular Republicans, Democrats, Whigs, and former Union soldiers into a Liberal Republican party. The hard work paid off in 1870 when Missourians voted to repeal the "Ironclad Oath." In 1875, a new constitution was adopted. When the people also elected Democrats and Liberal Republicans to Congress, it was clear that the state was ready to bury the hatreds caused by the war. Missouri turned toward the future with renewed optimism.

BANDITS IN MISSOURI

During the 1870s, western Missouri was jolted by an era of lawlessness. Many of the men who joined outlaw gangs had

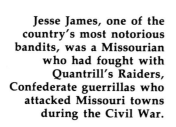

Jesse James, one of the country's most notorious bandits, was a Missourian who had fought with Quantrill's Raiders, Confederate guerrillas who attacked Missouri towns during the Civil War.

learned their gunfighting skills with Quantrill's Raiders, Confederate guerrillas who had attacked towns in Missouri during the Civil War. The names on the "wanted" posters included Belle Starr, the Younger brothers, and Sam Hildebrand.

The most notorious bandits were Jesse and Frank James. The James gang held up at least fourteen banks, robbed countless trains, and even held up the Kansas City Fair. Along the way, Jesse and his "boys" committed a number of murders. Finally, in 1882, Governor Thomas Crittenden offered a $10,000 reward for the James brothers. In April 1882, a member of the gang named Bob Ford claimed part of the reward by shooting Jesse from behind. The day of the bandits was ending, and by the end of that year, most of the outlaws were dead or had left the state.

THE GROWTH OF RAILROADING

Railroading got its start in Missouri when the Pacific Railroad built 5 miles (8 kilometers) of track between St. Louis and Cheltenham in 1852. Building the 125 miles (201 kilometers) of line to Jefferson City took another three years. The Civil War slowed progress, and it wasn't until 1865 that the railroad reached Kansas City. With every town demanding rail service, the railroads doubled the state's 900 miles (1,448 kilometers) of track over the next five years. The growth in traffic forced the railroads into a crash program to lay new track and to repair damage done during the Civil War.

Much of the construction was financed by railroad bonds backed by the state legislature, and the state ran up a debt of more than $31 million. Railroads also benefited from grants of federal land along their rights-of-way. Both the Pacific and the Hannibal and St. Joseph railroads received thousands of acres of land. The railroads made large profits by selling this land to farmers—who would later pay to ship their crops to market via the railroads.

Missouri's railroads opened up new markets in the East for the state's wheat, corn, and other products. Europe also was buying Missouri wheat, and the demand encouraged farmers to increase their acreage.

St. Louis almost lost its role as the nation's Gateway to the West during this age of railroad building. Chicago was emerging as the commercial and rail center of the Midwest. The railroads that came through Chicago to and from the West had railroad bridges across the upper Mississippi.

St. Louis asked one of America's great engineers, James Buchanan Eads, to build a bridge across the Mississippi. Eads rose to the challenge with a design for a magnificent two-level steel

The Charles H. Peck, which began operating in 1869, was the first locomotive of the Missouri Pacific Railroad Company.

bridge. Seven years in the building, the foundations of the Eads Bridge had to be set on bedrock, nearly 130 feet (40 meters) below the river's muddy bottom. When trains began chugging across the bridge in 1874, St. Louis regained its place as a railroad center.

POPULISM IN MISSOURI

Despite their new markets, the prices that farmers received for their crops fell sharply between 1865 and 1870. To combat this problem, Oliver Kelley formed a farmer's movement called the Patrons of Husbandry (commonly known as the Grange). The Grangers wanted lower shipping rates, lower prices for farm machinery, and lower interest rates on loans. By 1875, Missouri's branch of the Grange had more than two thousand chapters, the most of any state.

Using their political muscle, the Grangers tried to control railroad rates by pushing a series of laws through the General Assembly. After the laws were struck down by the United States Supreme Court in 1876, the Grange turned to Congress. The farmers' lobbying efforts paid off with the creation of the

Interstate Commerce Commission in 1887. It didn't happen overnight, but the ICC forced the railroads to set fair rates.

Missouri's Grangers also organized themselves as the People's Party. Better known as the Populists, the party supported limits on state debt, control of the railroads, improved schools, and expansion of the money supply. The initiative and referendum proposal, which allowed the people to propose new laws and vote for or against new laws, was sponsored by the Populists.

POLITICS AT THE TURN OF THE CENTURY

By the end of the 1800s, Missouri was playing a bigger role in national politics. In 1888, the Democratic National Convention met in St. Louis and nominated President Grover Cleveland for a second term. Cleveland carried Missouri, but Republican Benjamin Harrison won the election. In 1896, the Republicans brought their convention to St. Louis and nominated William McKinley of Ohio. Missourians voted for the Democratic candidate, William Jennings Bryan, but McKinley became president.

It was the Democrats' turn to meet at St. Louis in 1900. The convention hall, destroyed by fire in April, was rebuilt in time for the Democrats to nominate Bryan again. Once again, Missouri voted for the Democrat, and once again McKinley won the election.

During the 1890s, Missouri elected one of its ablest governors. William J. Stone took office just in time to steer the state through the financial panic of 1893. With tax revenues cut by 20 percent, the state faced a financial crisis. Thanks to Stone's strict economies, the state weathered the storm and actually paid off some of its bonds.

Chapter 6
INTO THE
TWENTIETH CENTURY

INTO THE TWENTIETH CENTURY

Meet me in St. Louis, Louis,
Meet me at the Fair.
Don't tell me the lights are shining
Anyplace but there.
We will dance the hootchie cootchie,
You will be my tootsie wootsie.
If you will meet me in St. Louis, Louis,
Meet me at the Fair!
—"Meet Me In St. Louis, Louis," by
Andrew B. Sterling and Kerry Mills

THE ST. LOUIS WORLD'S FAIR

In 1904, St. Louis played host to the biggest world's fair of its time. The exposition commemorated the purchase of the Louisiana Territory one hundred years earlier. From April 3 to December 1, people from all over the world were agreeing to "Meet Me in St. Louis," or "Looie," as a popular song advised. Fifteen large exhibition halls, plus special buildings sponsored by foreign governments, were built to house the exhibits. Visitors marveled at the displays in the Palace of Electricity, the Palace of Machinery, and the Palace of Forestry, Fish, and Game.

Twenty million people wandered through the fairground's site, which was decorated with statues, waterfalls, and a vast rose garden. Venetian gondolas ferried visitors across a lagoon, and people told time by a giant floral clock. The fair's rides and games were housed in an amusement zone called "The Pike."

Among the sights visitors beheld at the 1904 St. Louis World's Fair were the first flight of Captain Thomas Baldwin's dirigible, *California Arrow* (top left), and fifteen elaborate exposition halls, including the Palace of Education (left). They also sampled the newly invented ice-cream cones (above) and hot dogs.

The fair brought out the latest wonders of modern technology. People crowded in to view the first motion picture, wireless telegraphs, automatic dishwashers, and a display of one hundred automobiles. Fairgoers also sampled the newly invented ice-cream cones and hot dogs. When the fair closed, most of the temporary buildings were torn down, but a few were saved. The Palace of Fine Arts serves today as the St. Louis Art Museum.

During that same busy year, St. Louis played host to the Olympic Games. This was only the third modern Olympiad, following the rebirth of the games in Athens in 1896. The games were a triumph for the United States athletes, who won every gold medal in the track and field events.

JOSEPH FOLK AND "THE MISSOURI IDEA"

Joseph Folk, a young Tennessee lawyer who moved to St. Louis in the 1890s, was leader of a group of reform-minded Democrats called the Jefferson Club. He began speaking out about political corruption in the city. The message upset many Missourians, and they turned to Folk for leadership.

Folk told his listeners that politicians would not betray their trust if the people insisted on honesty in government. Folk's "Missouri Idea" was a restatement of one of Thomas Jefferson's principles: Honesty will always defeat wealth and special privilege. Folk's philosophy appealed to the voters, and they elected him governor in 1904. The new governor's honeymoon with the people didn't last long, however. Folk's popularity dropped when he tried to enforce laws against operating saloons and running dog races on Sunday.

When his fellow Democrats refused to support him, Folk said that he was the only honest politician in the state. A failure as a

Missouri native General John J. "Black Jack" Pershing led the American Expeditionary Forces (AEF), which fought in France against Germany during World War I.

governor, he lost his bid for the United States Senate in 1908. As Folk faded from public life, Republican Herbert Hadley captured the Jefferson City statehouse. This victory ended more than a quarter of a century of Democratic rule in Missouri.

MISSOURI IN WORLD WAR I

When the United States was drawn into World War I in 1917, Missouri's citizens threw themselves into the war effort. The state's own General John J. "Black Jack" Pershing led the American Expeditionary Forces' (AEF) doughboys who fought in France against Germany. The AEF included the Thirty-Fifth and Eighty-Ninth divisions, which were made up mostly of men from Missouri and Kansas. During the war, feelings ran high against the state's German American residents because people thought they might be disloyal. The schools stopped teaching German, and Berlin Avenue in St. Louis was renamed Pershing. More than 156,000 Missourians served in the armed forces during the war.

Missouri Senator James A. Reed giving a 1920 speech against United States participation in the League of Nations

THE JAMES REED ERA

After the defeat of Germany in World War I, most Missourians went back to their everyday pursuits. Along with the rest of the nation, many didn't want to be involved in the affairs of foreign countries. This feeling, called isolationism, surfaced in the opposition to an international peace-keeping body called the League of Nations. President Wilson wanted the Senate to approve the League treaty, but enough legislators—including

Missouri's James A. Reed—voted against it to defeat it. As a result, the United States did not join the League of Nations.

Reed served in the Senate from 1911 until his voluntary retirement in 1929. He was an outspoken opponent of government's tendency to interfere in people's lives. Reed opposed the drafting of soldiers in World War I, the prohibition of alcoholic beverages, and giving the vote to women. His attitude embarrassed Democratic leaders, who formed "Rid us of Reed" clubs. That didn't bother the voters back home, who gave him an easy election victory in 1922. Reed also enjoyed the support of the Pendergast machine in Kansas City.

A WELL-OILED POLITICAL MACHINE

Between the Civil War and World War II, many states saw the rise of powerful political machines. A "machine" is run by a political "boss," who dominates a city with the help of crooked politicians, labor leaders, and businessmen. The most powerful machine in Missouri was run by the Pendergast family of Kansas City. The family's rise to power began in 1892, when James Pendergast was elected to the city council. Tom Pendergast later took over his older brother's organization and turned it into a money-making machine.

The Pendergast machine rigged elections, controlled the police, and awarded city contracts to its friends. When Tom Pendergast approved a list of candidates, they were as good as elected. The residents of Kansas City knew about the machine, but accepted it as the price of living in a well-managed city. Pendergast's own income came from his concrete company and other businesses. Newcomers to Kansas City were always amazed by the city's generous use of concrete. Pendergast even paved the bed of Brush

Creek—at city expense. The machine ran out of steam in 1939 after Pendergast was sent to prison for tax evasion.

A MISSOURIAN MAKES GOOD IN WASHINGTON

Harry S. Truman, the first and only Missourian to become president of the United States, was born on a Missouri farm. During World War I he served as an artillery captain. When he returned home, he ran a men's hat and necktie shop until it failed in 1921. Truman then turned to politics. With the backing of the Pendergast machine, he was elected to a judgeship in the Jackson County Court. The job of a Missouri county judge in those days involved administrative work, not courtroom work. "Judge" Truman was defeated for reelection in 1924 but came back to win the post of presiding judge in 1926. He held the post for the next eight years. During that time, he earned a reputation for honesty and efficiency, even though the Pendergast machine was corrupt.

With Pendergast's help, Truman was elected to the United States Senate in 1934, during the Great Depression. As Missouri's junior senator, he supported President Franklin Delano Roosevelt's social programs and the rebuilding of the armed forces. After the United States entered World War II in 1941, Truman gained national attention for chairing a special committee that uncovered waste in defense spending. The reforms he pushed through saved at least $200 million.

WORLD WAR II

During the years of war against Japan, Germany, and Italy, 450,000 men and women from Missouri served in the armed forces. One of the army's outstanding generals, Omar Bradley,

Women workers at the Curtiss Wright airplane factory during World War II

was from Moberly, Missouri. General Bradley led the American forces that invaded Europe on D-Day in 1944.

The people who stayed home also did their share for the war effort. A committee for the war effort set a goal of 30,000 workers for war production, only to have more than 24,000 sign up in Kansas City alone. North American Aviation made Mitchell bombers in Kansas City, and the Darby shipyard at Kaw Point, on the Missouri River, produced a fleet of landing craft. The state's factories turned out everything from powdered eggs to TNT. By the end of the war, Missouri's workers had produced more than $4 billion worth of war supplies.

In 1944, with the war still raging, Roosevelt selected Truman to be his third vice-president. The new vice-president had been in office only eighty-three days when Roosevelt died. The "man from Missouri" was sworn in as president of the United States.

TRUMAN SURPRISES THE NATION

Many people predicted that Harry Truman would be a disaster as president. They made fun of his plain speech and his failure in the hat business. The record shows that Truman, an avid reader of history, was capable of making tough decisions—and making good ones.

It fell to Truman, for example, to make the decision to drop the atomic bomb on Japan. By ending the war quickly, historians believe, he saved more lives than were lost at Hiroshima and Nagasaki. A second tough call came when Truman saw that, after the war, the Russians were more interested in expanding their power than in maintaining world peace. To counter the Russian threat, Truman approved a huge program of foreign aid known as the Marshall Plan. The aid helped rebuild western Europe and kept the communists from taking over more countries. In addition, the Truman Doctrine promised United States military aid to any country that needed it to resist communism.

Truman ran for a second term in 1948 with predictions of certain defeat ringing in his ears. He responded by taking his campaign to the people. He spoke from the rear platform of his special train, and people came out to cheer, "Give 'em hell, Harry!" On election day, the voters handed Truman an upset victory over his Republican opponent, Thomas E. Dewey.

In June 1950, when communist North Korea invaded democratic South Korea, Truman acted with his usual swiftness. In addition to sending troops to Korea, he gained the support of the United Nations for the long war that followed. The Korean War ended in 1953 with South Korea still under a democratic form of government.

Although he could have run for a third term in 1952, Truman

This *Chicago Tribune* headline provided a laugh for President Harry S. Truman and the crowd that greeted him at St. Louis's Union Station after his election in 1948.

chose to retire. He and his wife, Bess, returned to Independence where they lived quietly until Truman died in 1972. During those last years, Truman worked in his presidential library and gave advice to any politician who stopped by to chat.

THE YEARS AFTER TRUMAN

Missouri joined in the electoral landslide that put Republican Dwight D. Eisenhower in the White House in 1952. In 1956, however, the state was one of the few that gave its electoral votes to the Democratic governor of Illinois, Adlai Stevenson. This was the first election since 1904 in which Missouri failed to vote for the winning presidential candidate.

In 1960, Missouri's Senator Stuart Symington was a native-son candidate for the Democratic nomination for president. He lost the nomination to John Kennedy, and Missouri helped Kennedy win his narrow victory over Richard Nixon. During the 1960s, Missouri's governor, John Dalton, pushed for state programs to attract new industries. St. Louis and Kansas City, however, slowed the governor's efforts by adopting earnings taxes. This is a tax that forces people who work in a city to pay for city services whether they live there or not. Despite the Republican victories in 1968 and 1972, Democrats kept control of Missouri's two Senate seats and all but one or two of its House seats.

In 1972, Missouri surprised the Democrats by electing its first Republican governor in twenty-eight years. Only thirty-three when he took office, Christopher "Kit" Bond also was the state's youngest governor. Also in 1972, voters passed a constitutional amendment that did away with two unpopular taxes—the taxes on household goods and bank deposits.

Large areas of the state were hit by the worst floods in history in 1973. At the peak of the flooding, 1.8 million acres (0.73 million hectares) in eighty-two of the state's counties were under water.

MISSOURI MOVES TOWARD THE 1990s

In 1976, the Republicans held their convention in Kansas City and nominated President Gerald Ford. Missouri, however, gave its electoral votes to the winner, Georgia's Jimmy Carter. That turned around in 1980, when the state returned to the Republican column and voted for Ronald Reagan. The election year was marked by a heat wave that killed more than three hundred people.

After voters put a spending lid on state government, Missouri ranked last in the amount it spent per capita on state services. For a time, the governor had to freeze state salaries and put off construction projects.

While the state fought out its money problems, a federal court ordered St. Louis to desegregate its schools. As a result of the ruling, students were bused between city and county schools, starting in 1981. Education got a boost in 1982 when the people voted an extra one-cent tax to support the schools.

In 1984, Missouri elected Harriett Woods as lieutenant governor. Woods was the first woman ever elected to statewide office in Missouri. The up-and-down economy of the state turned downward in 1986. Across the state, farmers were losing their land and rural businesses were failing. That same year, as a result of a court order, more aggressive efforts to reduce school segregation came to Kansas City.

PROTECTING THE ENVIRONMENT

Missouri works hard to protect its environment. The state has set aside more than 100,000 acres (40,470 hectares) for state parks and recreation areas. Many more thousands of acres are preserved as national parks and forests. Conservation agencies oversee almost fifty wildlife refuges. Deer and wild turkeys have been restored to areas where they were once almost extinct. To the delight of fish lovers, the state's lakes and streams are well stocked with crappie, trout, catfish, and smallmouth bass.

Though state and local governments try to enforce federal and state environmental laws, their budgets are limited. Pollution caused by industry remains one of the state's greatest environmental problems. Missouri is learning to cope with these problems, but federal, state, and local officials know they will have to work together to protect the state's quality of life.

By 1989, prosperity was returning to many parts of the state. Farmers were recovering from one of the worst droughts in history, and factories were hiring new workers. What will the twenty-first century bring? "Show me," say the Missourians. "We can handle it."

Chapter 7
GOVERNMENT AND THE ECONOMY

GOVERNMENT AND THE ECONOMY

The state seal of Missouri bears the Latin motto, *Salus populi suprema lex esto*. In English, it means, "Let the good of the people be the supreme law." The task of looking after "the good of the people" has been entrusted to Missouri's state, county, and local governments.

GOVERNMENT

Missouri's state government is divided among three branches: legislative, executive, and judicial. The legislative branch consists of a two-house legislature known as the General Assembly. The senate has 34 members, each of whom serves a four-year term. The 163 members of the house of representatives are elected to two-year terms. State laws are debated and passed by the General Assembly, which meets each January in Jefferson City, the state capital. This small city of 35,000 is located near the geographic center of Missouri.

Missouri's governor, who is elected to a four-year term, heads the executive branch. He is responsible for enforcing the law and administering state government. In 1960, voters approved an amendment to the 1945 constitution to allow governors to serve two consecutive terms. The voters also elect the lieutenant governor, secretary of state, attorney general, state treasurer, and state auditor. The governor appoints the heads of major departments.

The judicial branch is the Missouri court system. Circuit courts serve as trial courts for civil and criminal cases. Defendants who lose in the circuit courts can ask for hearings before the state courts of appeals. From there, cases can be appealed to the supreme court. The high court also serves as the final interpreter of the state's laws and constitution.

Missouri's 114 counties and its more than 3,100 local governments conduct their own affairs under charters approved by the legislature. St. Louis is classed as an independent city, which gives its city council the same powers as those held by county governments.

Local officials in most states guard their authority, but Missouri and Illinois know that problems don't stop at the state line. The two states have formed a development agency for the St. Louis metropolitan area. The superagency supervises sanitation, transportation, and other services on both sides of the river. In a similar manner, Missouri and Tennessee share the management of the bridges that connect those two states.

The people of Missouri pay taxes to support state and local governments. Taxes on income, sales, and gross business receipts are the biggest revenue raisers. The Missouri Lottery, which began in 1986, brings in some additional revenue. The state's total income of about $7.5 billion a year seldom stretches far enough to provide all the services the people want or need.

EDUCATION

Thanks to the constitution of 1820, Missouri's first free public schools were opened in 1839. Despite this quick start, Missourians were slow to spend money on their schools. Since the constitution of 1945 placed public education under a state department of

Washington University, in St. Louis

education, the state has been more generous. Missouri now spends about a third of its budget on its more than 2,000 public schools and more than 800,000 students.

When the University of Missouri at Columbia (UM-Columbia) opened in 1839, it was the first state university west of the Mississippi. Many of the school's 22,000 students are attracted to the School of Journalism. This training ground for reporters and editors was the first of its kind when it opened in 1908. The school's College of Agriculture reaches out to students in rural areas with special extension classes. Another branch of the University of Missouri, located at Rolla, specializes in technical and engineering courses. Both UM-Columbia and UM-Rolla have major nuclear research centers. The other two UM campuses are located in St. Louis and Kansas City.

In addition to the four campuses of the state university system, Missouri has a college or university for almost any interest. There are more than thirty private colleges and universities, plus junior colleges, Bible schools, technical schools, and art and music schools. Some of them are very old. Stephens College, which

About half of Missouri's cultivated land is planted in soybeans (above), the state's leading field crop.

enrolls only women, first opened its doors in 1833. St. Louis University, a Catholic school, was founded in 1818 and became a university in 1832. In 1853, Washington University (now well known for its excellent medical school) was founded by Dr. William Eliot as a seminary.

For Missouri's readers, there are seventy-nine county and sixteen regional library systems. Bookmobiles operate throughout the state, serving people who don't have access to other libraries. In addition to the public and university libraries, the state has a number of special collections. The Harry S. Truman Library at Independence attracts visitors and researchers from all over the world. In Columbia, the State Historical Society has put together a valuable collection of rare books, journals, maps, newspapers, and paintings.

Pigs (above), beef cattle (left), and other livestock
produce more than half of Missouri's farm income.

AGRICULTURE

Missouri's varied soils and favorable climate allow its farmers
to grow a wide range of crops. More than 70 percent of the state's
land area is used for farming. The richest soil is found north of the
Missouri River and in the bottomlands of the Bootheel. Roughly
half of the cultivated land is planted in soybeans. Missouri's
farmers also harvest corn, wheat, cotton, hay, tobacco, rice, grapes,
pecans, and many other crops. Dairy and beef cattle, horses,
mules, pigs, and other livestock produce more than half of
Missouri's farm income.

Most of Missouri's farmers raise both livestock and field crops,
instead of depending on a single product. Each region tends to
specialize, however. Soybeans are king in the southeast and

McDonnell Douglas, of St. Louis, manufactures military aircraft, commercial jets, and electronic equipment for customers all over the world. These workers are assembling jet fighter planes.

northwest. The fertile fields of the Bootheel, by contrast, produce millions of dollars' worth of cotton every year. Corn and wheat grow well in central and north-central Missouri, and the Ozarks produce hay and good pastureland for livestock. Corn and cattle do well north of the Missouri, while the southwest profits from one of the nation's largest feeder-pig industries.

Missouri's farms are decreasing in number but growing in size. In 1960, the state's 180,000 farms averaged 193 acres (78 hectares). By 1986, the number had fallen to 114,000 farms, but the typical size had increased to 268 acres (108.5 hectares). Even so, Missouri has the second-greatest number of farms in the United States. Only Texas has more.

BUSINESS AND MANUFACTURING

Many people think of Missouri as a farm state, but business and manufacturing generate more income and more jobs. More than 410,000 Missourians work in over 7,000 factories, making everything from space hardware to corncob pipes. Another 1.5 million people carry on the public and private business of the state. More than 300,000 men and women work for state and local

St. Louis is the home of Anheuser-Busch, the world's largest brewery and a historical landmark.

governments, for example, and another 500,000 have jobs in the retail sales and service sector.

The list of Missouri's major companies reads like a list of "Who's Who in the Business World." McDonnell Douglas Corporation of St. Louis makes military aircraft, commercial jets, and electronic equipment for customers all over the world. American astronauts flew into orbit in the company's Mercury and Gemini space capsules. St. Louis is also the home of Anheuser-Busch, the world's largest brewery. In addition to producing jets and beer, Missouri ranks second in the nation in the production of automobiles. Chrysler, Ford, and General Motors all have assembly plants in or near St. Louis and Kansas City. Other major manufacturers are Monsanto (chemicals), Hallmark (greeting cards), and Ralston Purina (livestock feed and cereals).

Blessed with a central location and abundant natural resources, Missouri attracts more than 60 new plants and creates more than 4,500 new jobs each year. The rapid growth has benefited many of the state's smaller cities. Instead of limiting their activity to St. Louis and Kansas City, companies are turning cities such as Springfield, St. Joseph, and Columbia into beehives of activity.

Crushed stone, especially limestone, contributes greatly to the state's economy. This limestone mine is in Springfield.

NATURAL RESOURCES

Ever since 1720, when Philip Renault opened the first mine near Fredericktown, Missouri has been a major producer of lead. Today, Missouri produces over 85 percent of the nation's supply of this useful metal. In addition, Missouri leads the nation in producing fire clay, and is a leading producer of lime, barite, zinc, cement, and copper.

Missouri's mines add about $1 billion to the state's economy each year. The biggest moneymakers are lead, cement, crushed stone, and coal. In an age of open-pit mining, the Pea Ridge Iron Ore Company operates the only underground iron mine still active in the country. Cobalt is another Missouri product. White Carthage marble and red granite are quarried in Missouri and sold to builders all over the country.

Forest products are another important natural resource. Much of the forested area is found in the Ozarks, where loggers harvest pine, oak, walnut, and hickory trees. The state supports nearly two thousand industries that produce such wood products as charcoal, lumber, and barrels. Careless logging practices once threatened to destroy Missouri's forests, but new trees now are being planted faster than old ones are cut down.

TRANSPORTATION

Missouri has been a transportation hub for more than two hundred years. Before roads and railroads were built, the Ohio, Missouri, and Mississippi rivers were America's highways to the heart of the continent. Today, the heavy barges that move slowly up and down the Missouri and Mississippi rivers have turned St. Louis into one of the nation's busiest inland ports.

Passenger and freight trains crisscross the state on 8,000 miles (12,874 kilometers) of track, and St. Louis and Kansas City are among the nation's busiest rail centers. The road network also carries a heavy traffic load. Missouri has more than 9,000 miles (14,484 kilometers) of major highways and more than 100,000 miles (160,930 kilometers) of all-weather roads. Airplanes fly out of more than three hundred airports, including Lambert Airport in St. Louis and Kansas City International Airport.

COMMUNICATION

Missouri's first newspaper, the *Missouri Gazette*, hit the streets in 1808. Today, about 50 daily newspapers and 250 weeklies bring news and entertainment to the people of the state. The *St. Louis Post-Dispatch*, the *Kansas City Times*, and the *Kansas City Star* are among the nation's leading newspapers. Joseph Pulitzer, the founder of the *Post-Dispatch*, is best remembered for establishing the Pulitzer Prizes. Writers who earn Pulitzers know they've reached the top of their profession.

Radio broadcasting began in 1921 when experimental station WEW went on the air from St. Louis University. Today, the state has about 220 AM and FM radio stations. Television viewers can choose from 25 local television stations, as well as cable systems.

Chapter 8
CULTURE AND RECREATION

CULTURE AND RECREATION

The whole world knows Missouri's best-loved writer, the immortal Samuel Clemens, better known as Mark Twain. What non-Missourians may not know is that the state also produces fine painting, architecture, and music. Working in their own original styles, the state's artists have recorded the spirit of a people and their colorful history.

ART

The first well-known painter of Missouri life was George Catlin. In 1830, the young artist went west to record on canvas the Indian way of life. Catlin had seen the crude paintings brought back by the Lewis and Clark expedition and thought the Indians deserved better. General William Clark arranged for Catlin to visit Missouri, Iowa, and Osage tribes, along with many others. During his time in Missouri, Catlin made sketches, took notes, and collected Indian clothing and weapons. The Indians made him feel welcome, and the artist learned to respect their customs. Back in his St. Louis studio, Catlin turned his sketches into finished paintings. Along with his portraits of Indian chiefs, he painted the excitement of the buffalo hunt, the fury of a prairie fire, and the everyday life of an Indian camp. Catlin created a priceless record of a now-vanished way of life.

George Caleb Bingham captured Missouri's river frontier on canvas before it, too, disappeared. Bingham was eight years old in

Missouri's best-loved writer, Samuel Clemens (better known as Mark Twain), in front of his boyhood home in Hannibal

1819 when his family moved to Franklin in the Boone's Lick area of Missouri. The raw life of the frontier town fascinated the boy. As he wandered the streets, he saw Osage warriors, traveling preachers, riverboat sailors, and fur trappers. Bingham filed these images away in his head and began his art career by copying the pictures he saw in books. That was the best he could do because there weren't any art schools west of the Mississippi.

By 1834, Bingham was earning his living as a portrait painter in Columbia. Six years later, the young artist opened a studio in Washington, D.C., and began to paint the West of his boyhood. He captured the people and the land in vivid color and superb detail. The artist was elected to the Missouri legislature in 1848 and served as state treasurer from 1862 to 1865. Today, tourists can visit Bingham's restored home at Arrow Rock State Park, east of Kansas City.

One of Missouri's great characters was muralist Thomas Hart Benton. The artist's great-uncle, also named Thomas Hart Benton, had been one of the state's first United States senators. Benton the artist was no politician. He was a down-to-earth man who loved whiskey, chewed tobacco, and argued with art critics, politicians, and other artists. After serving in World War I and teaching in New York, Benton completed his first mural in 1931. The vigorous, rounded figures caught the art world's fancy. He was hired to paint murals at the Whitney Museum of American Art and at the Century of Progress World's Fair in Chicago.

In 1935, Benton returned to his home state to paint a mural in the house lounge of the Missouri State Capitol. The stormy artist refused to paint an idealized history peopled with heroic pioneers. In his mural, truthful as always, he included political boss Tom Pendergast, bandit Jesse James, and Mark Twain's Huckleberry Finn. Some politicians wanted to cover the offending wall with whitewash but cooler heads saved the mural. Benton went on painting in his robust style for another forty years.

FROM GREEK REVIVAL TO MODERN SKYSCRAPERS

The frontier was disappearing by the time Missouri became a state in 1821. Wealthy citizens wanted fine homes, and state politicians wanted impressive public buildings. The architects of the day were influenced by a style called Greek Revival. They designed stately plantation homes and decorated the front porches with Greek columns. By the time the third state capitol was built in 1917, the style had shifted. Along with rows of tall columns, the marble building was topped with a graceful Roman dome.

Missouri architect George Ingham Barnett designed the 1871 Renaissance Revival Governor's Mansion in Jefferson City. The

Country Club Plaza, in Kansas City, was the nation's first shopping center.

building's four pink granite columns were a gift from a former governor.

After architect Louis Sullivan built the first modern skyscraper in Chicago, he came to St. Louis in 1890 to design the Wainwright Building. Turn-of-the-century Missourians were awed by the spectacular ten-story building, now recognized as one of Sullivan's finest works. Kansas City didn't have the state's first skyscraper, but it built the nation's first shopping center. The Kansas City Country Club Plaza, designed with Spanish fountains and tree-lined walks, opened in 1920.

Frank Lloyd Wright, another giant of modern architecture, rejected the idea of massive skyscrapers. Wright believed that a building should look as though it "grew" naturally out of its site. Kansas City has three examples of Wright's work—the Clarence Sondern home, the Frank Bott home, and the Kansas City Community Christian Church. Built in 1940, the church's long, low lines look as up-to-date as when Wright designed it.

Musician Scott Joplin, the master of ragtime, got his start in Sedalia, where he played piano and wrote music for eleven years.

Eero Saarinen's Gateway Arch, completed in 1965, opened a new age in architecture for St. Louis. The stainless steel arch, one of the century's great engineering feats, provides a fine view of the city's new buildings. The most notable designs include the fifteen-story headquarters of Pet, Inc.; the Clarion Hotel, with its revolving restaurant; and architect Gyo Obata's Priory Chapel.

MUSIC AND THE OTHER LIVELY ARTS

The mention of Missouri music brings jazz to mind. That's as it should be, because Scott Joplin, the master of ragtime, got his start in Sedalia. He played piano and wrote music there for eleven years. "The Entertainer" and other Joplin pieces gained millions of new fans in 1973 when they were used in the hit movie *The Sting*. Most jazz fans also remember two classic tunes with St. Louis in the title—W. C. Handy's "St. Louis Blues" and Tom Turpin's "St. Louis Rag." Egbert Van Alstyne added "In the Shade of the Old Apple Tree," a song that became an enduring favorite.

From concerts played by the St. Louis Symphony to gospel music and country-and-western, Missourians can choose the type of music they like best. Country music, for example, is popular in the area around Branson, in southwestern Missouri. Those who like mountain music head for the Baldknobbers Hillbilly Jamboree Show. Country-and-western fans prefer the Branson Opry House.

One thing is certain. In Missouri, the hills—and the plains and the cities—are alive with music.

SPORTS

Missouri sports fans cheer for a variety of teams. Baseball, football, soccer, and basketball are all represented in the state.

In eastern Missouri, baseball means the National League's St. Louis Cardinals. In 1987, more than three million fans turned out to cheer the Cardinals to the National League pennant. The "Redbirds" lost the World Series, however, four games to three. That loss didn't hit the city's pride quite as hard as the World Series of 1985 did. That was the year the Kansas City Royals beat the Cardinals in an all-Missouri series. Despite those two losses, St. Louis has a long history of World Series victories. The team has won nine world championships over the years.

The Cardinals play in 54,000-seat Busch Stadium, which also houses the St. Louis Sports Hall of Fame. Some of the Cardinals remembered in the museum also won the National League's Most

The National League St. Louis Cardinals play in Busch Stadium (foreground), which also houses the St. Louis Sports Hall of Fame.

Valuable Player (MVP) awards. The list includes names that every baseball fan knows by heart—Dizzy Dean (1934), Stan Musial (1948), Orlando Cepeda (1967), Bob Gibson (1968), and Willie McGee (1985).

The Kansas City Royals play baseball in the 40,000-seat Truman Sports Complex, built in 1972. The Royals, who compete in the American League, lost their first World Series appearance to Philadelphia in 1980. The team made up for that loss with its 1985 victory over their cross-state rivals from St. Louis. Royals batting champion George Brett was named MVP of the American League in 1980 when he hit a classy .390.

St. Louis lost its National Football League team when the Cardinals moved to Phoenix in 1988. The Kansas City Chiefs, who play in 78,000-seat Arrowhead Stadium, are now the state's only professional football team. The Chiefs have had a losing record in recent years, but they have made two trips to the Super Bowl. In 1967, the Chiefs lost the first Super Bowl to the Green Bay Packers, 35-10. Three years later, the team won Super Bowl IV by beating the Minnesota Vikings, 23-7.

Missouri also supports pro teams in hockey and indoor soccer. The St. Louis Blues, who compete in the National Hockey League, play about forty home games each year. On the other side of the state, the Kansas City Comets play the fast and exciting sport of indoor soccer.

Many sports fans divide their loyalties between the pro teams and the University of Missouri-Columbia Tigers. The university men's teams compete in all major college sports, including football, basketball, swimming, and gymnastics. The Lady Tigers play a similarly full schedule of games, except for football. The university competes in the tough Big Eight Conference against teams from Colorado, Iowa State, Kansas, Kansas State, Nebraska, Oklahoma, and Oklahoma State. The teams from the state's smaller universities and colleges don't earn as many headlines, but fans fill their stadiums and arenas as well.

OUTDOOR FUN AT EVERY TURN

One problem with taking a vacation in Missouri is that there are so many places to go and so many things to do. The state's parks, lakes, rivers, caves, and woods provide some of the best outdoor recreation in the nation.

Vacationers who want to "go with the flow" head for one of Missouri's rivers. River sports include canoeing, fishing, houseboating, rafting, and floating. Floating may be the simplest, most relaxing sport ever invented. The "floater" pumps up an old inner tube, packs some food in a waterproof bag, and drifts downstream on a lazy current. Other floaters prefer to do their drifting in canoes, on rafts, or in kayaks.

Some favorite stretches of river for floating include the Ozark National Scenic Riverways, the Current and Jacks Fork rivers,

Water sports of all kinds are popular in Missouri. These sunbathers and swimmers are enjoying Johnson Shut-ins State Park, in Big Springs Country (above), and a fisherman shows off his white bass catch at Lake of the Ozarks (right).

Shoal Creek, the North Fork, and the Meramec River. Anyone who wants more luxury can take a river cruise on a steamboat or riverboat. Cruises leave from St. Louis, Kansas City, St. Charles, Hannibal, and other river ports.

Fishing enthusiasts can choose from nearly a million acres (more than 400,000 hectares) of water. This includes about 50,000 miles (80,500 kilometers) of rivers and streams. These varied waters provide an ideal habitat for almost two hundred species of fish. The giant river catfish are a favorite catch, along with crappie, trout, sunfish, walleye, and bass. The record fish taken in the state was a Missouri blue catfish that weighed a whopping 117 pounds (53 kilograms).

Missouri's lakes are wonderful playgrounds. People visit the lakes to swim, sail, scuba dive, and water-ski. Some of the state's lakes have shoreline marinas, campgrounds, and other facilities.

One of Missouri's largest lakes is Lake of the Ozarks, located in the central part of the state. This huge lake has more than two

Canoeists on the Current River, in the Ozarks

hundred resorts along its shoreline. Also popular are Table Rock
Lake (in the southwest), Clearwater Lake (in the southeast), Bull
Shoals Lake (on the Missouri-Arkansas border), and Mark Twain
Lake (in the northeast). Set amid rolling hills and rocky bluffs,
Mark Twain is the state's newest lake.

Missouri encourages its residents and visitors to enjoy the
state's excellent hunting. The state sells hunting licenses for deer,
turkeys, rabbits, squirrels, game birds, ducks, and geese. Hunters
also stalk less common game, including raccoons, beavers, foxes,
and opossums. For those who don't like to hunt, the woodlands
offer camping, hiking, cycling, backpacking, and birdwatching.

The state's many caves provide a different type of vacation
experience. Some of the caves have a history that goes back two
thousand years, to the time when they were used by Indians. In
the 1800s, Meramec Caverns, near Stanton, sheltered escaping slaves
who were traveling the Underground Railway. It also served as a
powder dump for Union forces during the Civil War, and later

Children enjoy the Oceans of Fun water park in Kansas City.

was used as a hideout by Jesse James. Today, about two dozen of Missouri's caves are open to visitors. Guided tours take people through twisting tunnels and into lighted caverns where they can enjoy the timeless beauty of this underground world.

AMUSEMENT PARKS AND FESTIVALS

When people tire of floating, camping, and fishing, they can turn to other forms of recreation. Missouri has hundreds of golf courses and thousands of tennis courts. Family fun parks, such as Six Flags Over Mid-America (St. Louis), Worlds of Fun (Kansas City), and Silver Dollar City (Branson), offer fast rides, musical shows, water slides, and historical exhibits.

All through the year, Missouri celebrates with a variety of festivals and fairs. In August, horse lovers turn out for the Bootheel Rodeo at Sikeston, the state's largest. Music festivals feature every form of music from classical to jazz, ragtime, and bluegrass. St. Louis claims that its V. P. (Veiled Prophet) Fair is the nation's largest Fourth of July celebration. Kansas City

The Kodak Hot-Air Balloon Festival, in St. Louis

counters with its St. Patrick's Day parade, one of the three largest in the country.

Summer is fair time, and visitors can choose from more than two hundred local and regional fairs. The grandest fair of all is the Missouri State Fair at Sedalia. Large or small, the fairs display the produce and livestock raised on local farms and sell homemade food and craft items. Fairgoers crowd the grounds to see tractor pulls, stock car races, and big-name musicians.

Some festivals give Missourians a chance to win medals. The annual Show-Me State Games in Columbia, for example, bring together athletes of all ages and abilities for three summer days of Olympic-style competition. Columbia also plays host to the Missouri State Old-Time Fiddling Championship each October.

Missourians should never be bored. In one busy day in St. Louis, visitors can tour the Anheuser-Busch Brewery, the Missouri Botanical Garden, the zoo, and the National Bowling Hall of Fame. All across the state, there are pageants, concerts, and historical sites. In Missouri, the problem isn't one of wondering what to do. The problem lies in deciding what to do next!

Chapter 9

A WHIRLWIND TOUR OF THE SHOW ME STATE

A WHIRLWIND TOUR OF THE SHOW ME STATE

Missouri is a land with a multitude of choices. In a single day, a visitor can ride on a steamboat, tour an aerospace factory, and visit a fine zoo. Anyone who tires of busy, modern cities can escape to open farmland and peaceful country towns. A family can fish on quiet lakes, hike across Ozark hills, and find adventure in dimly lighted caves.

It would take years to see everything that Missouri has to offer. Here is a zigzag tour that crosses the state and takes in some of its most interesting sights.

ST. LOUIS

St. Louis was a success almost from the day that Pierre Laclède picked the site for his fur-trading post. As America's Gateway to the West, the town grew and prospered. Today, a Carl Milles sculpture, *The Meeting of the Waters,* stands outside Union Station. The sculpture is a reminder of the city's location near the meeting place of the Missouri and Mississippi rivers.

Although St. Louis was founded by the French, later settlers included large numbers of German, English, Italian, Scottish, African American, and Hispanic immigrants. Each group of immigrants brought their own religious and cultural traditions with them. Today, almost half a million Missourians make their home in this cosmopolitan city. During the 1970s, however, the

Sculptor Carl Milles designed the *Meeting of the Waters* fountain that stands in front of the Union Station complex in St. Louis.

city lost its title as the largest city on the Mississippi. Both Memphis and New Orleans surpassed St. Louis in population. When the suburbs are included, metropolitan St. Louis has a population of more than 2.3 million.

To visitors, St. Louis is a fascinating mix of new and old. Glass-walled skyscrapers rise above blocks of townhouses that were built in the 1870s. The St. Louis Art Museum is housed in a striking building left over from the 1904 World's Fair. Near the river, in the shadow of the Gateway Arch, the Old Courthouse tells another historic story. This was the scene of the legal battle over slavery known as the Dred Scott case. The modern St. Louis Science Center, by contrast, provides a planetarium, displays of ancient fossils, and the latest in robotics.

Along the river, old levees lined with cobblestones still protect the city from spring floods. Behind them, run-down warehouses serve as a reminder of the urban decay that once nibbled at

The Climatron, at the Missouri Botanical Garden in St. Louis

St. Louis. After years of neglect, city leaders began one of the nation's largest and most expensive programs of urban renewal in the 1960s. Today, a billion dollars later, the Gateway Arch stands as a soaring symbol of the city's new energy. The arch is the centerpiece of the Jefferson National Expansion Memorial. Trams carry visitors up the hollow legs of the arch to the enclosed observation deck, 630 feet (192 meters) above the city. Beneath the arch, the underground Museum of Westward Expansion reminds visitors of the hardships faced by the early settlers.

Not far from the arch is a rebuilt downtown that features elegant stores, luxury hotels, and fine apartment buildings. Two St. Louis landmarks are the modern Cervantes Convention Center and Busch Stadium, home of baseball's St. Louis Cardinals. Both the convention center and the stadium were built with private funds. Leaving the riverside area, Lindell Boulevard leads to the eighty-year-old Cathedral of St. Louis. Art experts believe that its collection of mosaics ranks with the best in Europe.

Many visitors are drawn to St. Louis by its active cultural life. Jazz fans identify the city with the music of W. C. Handy, who wrote his famous "St. Louis Blues" in 1914. Today, St. Louis takes pride in its fine symphony orchestra, a fifteen-thousand-seat open-air amphitheater for opera, a well-managed zoo, and one of the world's oldest botanical gardens.

COLUMBIA

The quiet university town of Columbia likes to call itself the "Athens of Missouri." It is an easy drive west from St. Louis on Interstate 70. Founded in 1819, Columbia served as a supply center for pioneers moving west on the Boone's Lick Trail. Many of the town's old homes are built in the southern plantation style.

Today, the town's sixty thousand inhabitants welcome more than twenty-two thousand students to its University of Missouri campus. Six Ionic columns—all that remain of the university's first building—are a major Columbia landmark. Visitors can tour the university and take in the exhibits at the State Historical Society. Anyone who wants to meet a Missouri mule should head for the experimental farm run by the School of Agriculture. The school keeps mules "for old times' sake."

Columbia is more than a college town, however. The city serves as a regional center for health care and several statewide organizations and insurance companies make their headquarters there. Shelter Gardens, at the Shelter Insurance Company, displays many types of flowers as well as more than three hundred varieties of trees and shrubs. Also on the grounds is a fragrance garden for the blind.

MEXICO

The drive northeast from Columbia to the small town of Mexico passes over narrow backcountry roads. Here, near the Salt River on the upland prairie, Mexico has been the home of fine horses for 150 years. By 1908, the trotting and pacing races at Mexico's annual fair were offering the highest purses (prize money) in the nation—as much as $1,500. Today, the racetracks are gone and the breeders raise saddle horses for the spring and fall auctions. The American Saddle Horse Museum, housed in a Civil-War-era home called Graceland, is a popular stop for visitors.

Mexico is also home to the Missouri Military Academy. During the school term, visitors turn out to watch the top-rated military academy's cadets march in review.

HANNIBAL

From Mexico, a good highway leads visitors farther northeast to the sleepy Mississippi River town of Hannibal. Millions of Americans who have never been to Missouri feel they know Hannibal through the books of Samuel Langhorne Clemens. Better known as Mark Twain, Clemens lived in Hannibal from 1839 until 1857. It was in Hannibal that Clemens laid the scenes for the adventures of Tom Sawyer and Huckleberry Finn. His boyhood home on Hill Street still stands beside the famous whitewashed fence and the Mark Twain Museum. The fence is the scene of the National Fence Painting Contest in July.

Everything about Hannibal reminds visitors of its Mark Twain heritage. Guided tours of Becky Thatcher's house and the Mark Twain Cave are offered throughout the year. In the afternoon, the four-hundred-passenger Mark Twain Excursion Boat casts off for

TOM SAWYER'S FENCE
HERE STOOD THE BOARD
FENCE WHICH TOM SAWYER
PERSUADED HIS GANG TO
PAY HIM FOR THE PRIVILEGE
OF WHITEWASHING. TOM
SAT BY AND SAW THAT IT
WAS WELL DONE

The whitewashed fence made famous by Mark Twain stands beside Twain's boyhood home in Hannibal, and a statue of Tom Sawyer and Huckleberry Finn has been erected at the foot of Cardiff Hill.

a one-hour voyage on the Mississippi. Life-size statues of Tom and Huck can be seen at the foot of Cardiff Hill, along with a fine view of the bluffs above the river. Hannibal is now a modern town, but it somehow keeps the feeling of the 1840s. If someone were to yell, "Steeeeeemboat's a'comin' round the bend!" people might come running just as they did in Samuel Clemens's time.

ST. JOSEPH

Two hundred miles (322 kilometers) of straight, fast highway leads across northern Missouri's prosperous dairy and cattle farms from Hannibal to St. Joseph. Now the state's fifth-largest city, "St. Joe" began as an Indian trading post in 1826. During the 1840s, the town on the Missouri River was a popular starting point for settlers on their way to Oregon. By the end of that decade, up to twenty steamboats a day were picking up furs and buffalo hides for the St. Louis market. Slaughterhouses were opened to supply the Gold Rush pioneers with meat, and meat packing is still one of the city's main industries.

**The Pony Express statue
in St. Joseph**

Most visitors to St. Joseph want to see the Jesse James Home and the Pony Express Stables Museum. Jesse James was a well-known outlaw who "retired" in St. Joseph, only to be shot for a $5,000 reward by a former member of his gang. The James Home has some of the outlaw's possessions on display, and features a bullet hole in one wall. The Pony Express exhibits are housed in the stables that served as the eastern end of the service during 1860 and 1861.

KANSAS CITY

The traffic between St. Joseph and Kansas City zips past prosperous farms and well-kept pastures. Many visitors to Kansas City think of the words "Everything's up-to-date in Kansas City," from the musical *Oklahoma!* That's still true today. Kansas City ranks first in the nation as a farm-market center. This booming, well-planned Missouri River city has more statues on its tree-lined streets than do most European capitals.

The Kansas City skyline from Penn Valley Park

The town was founded in 1821, and during the 1840s, steamboat traffic on the Missouri turned Kansas City into a major trading center. It was also the last stop for settlers and gold seekers heading west. By 1900, Kansas City was the center of the country's cattle market. People knew that steaks stamped "Kansas City Beef" were the best the nation could produce. The city grew rapidly during World War I, driven by the growing demand for midwestern beef, wheat, and corn. Meat packing and flour milling expanded, and industry arrived to balance the region's agricultural economy. During the Great Depression of the 1930s, when other cities were barely surviving, Kansas City began a ten-year rebuilding plan. World War II brought another wave of rapid growth.

Kansas City is the hub of a metropolitan region of more than 1.3 million people. The city's twin—Kansas City, Kansas—lies just across a street called State Line Road. Greater Kansas City spreads across seven Missouri and Kansas counties.

Kansas City is home to more than two hundred of the country's largest industrial firms. Many are tied to agriculture, while others assemble autos and trucks, process food, and fabricate metals. On the floor of the Board of Trade, brokers buy and sell millions of bushels of wheat every day. Deep under the city lies one of the country's three foreign-trade zones. There, in a maze of caverns, imported goods are stored free of dust until they're sold and distributed.

In addition to its business and industry, Kansas City is proud of its ultramodern airport, the $200-million Crown Center, and the Harry S. Truman Sports Complex. The Crown Center is a city within a city, with acres of stores, offices, and apartments. Developed by Hallmark Cards, it is one of the nation's largest private urban-renewal projects. The sports complex features the world's only twin baseball and football stadiums.

There's always something to do in Kansas City. Swope Park offers fishing, boating, and the Kansas City Zoo. For artistic tastes, the city offers orchestra concerts, Indian exhibits at the Museum of History and Science, and a tour of the home of muralist Thomas Hart Benton. In November, Kansas City puts on the American Royal Livestock, Horse Show and Rodeo. This popular event has been held since 1899 and draws exhibitors from all over the country.

INDEPENDENCE

A short drive east from downtown Kansas City takes visitors to Missouri's fourth-largest city—Independence. In 1821, Independence was one of the starting points for the Santa Fe Trail,

President Harry S. Truman and his wife, Bess, lived in this white Victorian house in Independence from 1919 until their deaths.

and in the 1840s, the trails to Oregon and California began here. The city celebrates its pioneer past during Santa-Cali-Gon Days on Labor Day weekend. The festival features carnival rides, Old West shoot-outs, a fiddler's contest, and bluegrass music.

In this century, Independence gained fame as the hometown of President Harry S. Truman. The Harry S. Truman Library displays his official papers and features a replica of the White House office. One prized display is the document of surrender that ended World War II, signed by Japanese diplomats on the deck of the USS *Missouri*. A highlight of any trip to Independence is a visit to the white Victorian house in which the president and his wife, Bess, lived from 1919 until their deaths. The Trumans are buried side by side in the courtyard of the Truman Library. Also open to visitors is Truman's office in the Jackson County Courthouse.

A statue of Thomas Jefferson stands in front of the capitol building in Jefferson City.

JEFFERSON CITY

From Independence, a trip of 140 miles (225 kilometers) through the center of Missouri leads to the state capital. Jefferson City lies on the south bank of the Missouri River. Where Creole flatboats once floated, the river now carries barges, tugboats, and tourist steamers. The main business of Jefferson City, however, is state government. With only 35,000 inhabitants, it is one of the smallest of all the state capitals.

The imposing state capitol building stands on a bluff high above the Missouri. The first two capitols were destroyed by fire, and the present capitol was finished in 1917. Built of white marble quarried in Carthage, Missouri, the building was modeled after Pennsylvania's state capitol. In the house lounge, Thomas Hart Benton's murals tell the colorful story of the state's history. Elsewhere in the capitol, other murals depict Missouri's legends and landscape.

JOPLIN

Joplin, in the southwest corner of Missouri, lies on rolling prairie at the edge of the Ozark Highlands. A network of abandoned mine tunnels honeycombs the ground under the city, a reminder of its days as a lead-mining center. In the 1800s, pure lead lay so close to the surface that it was sometimes exposed by hard rains. The first serious mining efforts began in 1849. The city's mining heritage can be seen at the Tri-State Mineral Museum, where scale models of lead-mining equipment are on display.

The Dorothea B. Hoover Historical Museum brings back the nineteenth century, with period furnishings, miniature displays, and even a Victorian dollhouse. The Taylor Performing Arts Center and original buildings from Mission Hills Farm are part of the Missouri Southern State College campus. Nearby streams offer excellent fishing. Not far from town is the George Washington Carver National Monument.

SPRINGFIELD

The drive eastward from Joplin takes visitors to Springfield, Missouri's third-largest city and the southwestern gateway to the Ozarks. Springfield developed as a stopping place for families on their way west. Several Civil War battles were fought in the area, and the dead from both armies are buried in Springfield's National Cemetery.

Although it has five colleges and a solid industrial base, Springfield is best known for recreation. Adventurous visitors can take a tram ride through Fantastic Caverns, one of Missouri's biggest caves. The exhibits at the Museum of the Ozarks' History, by contrast, tell the quiet story of life in Springfield during the 1800s. Best of all, Springfield is only a short drive from marvelous fishing, boating, and hiking facilities at Fellows, McDaniel, and Springfield lakes.

THROUGH THE OZARKS TO NEW MADRID

The trip from Springfield southeast to New Madrid takes visitors through the heart of the Ozarks. The eastward journey leads through forests of oak and pine, past rushing streams, and through deep-cut valleys. When the road leaves the Ozarks, it flattens out to cross the cotton fields of the Alluvial Plain. The small town of New Madrid lies at the end of the road, nestled against the Mississippi at New Madrid Bend. Here, the river loops back on itself in an almost 360-degree curve.

New Madrid began as a trading post in 1783, and settlers arrived six years later. The road the Spanish called *El Camino Real* ran through the town. Today, that route is known as Interstate 55. New Madrid's growth was halted by the massive earthquakes that hit in 1811 and 1812. Fields and orchards split open and forests were swallowed up by surging river water. Luckily, only a few people were injured. Today, the Historical Museum's exhibits recapture that vanished age of earthquakes, steamboats, and the bombardment by Union forces during the Civil War. The Hunter-Dawson Home State Historic Site in New Madrid is an antebellum mansion built in 1858.

STE. GENEVIEVE

Heading north along *El Camino Real*, the road leads to Ste. Genevieve, the oldest permanent settlement in Missouri. The

The French Colonial Bolduc House, in Ste. Genevieve, has been restored to its 1770 condition.

small town once rivaled St. Louis in size, but today it has retired to a quieter lifestyle. The townspeople treasure their French Creole buildings and their old customs. The bells of the church ring a call to prayer three times a day. Du Bourg Place, at the center of town, is bordered by well-kept homes and pink-walled gardens.

Descendants of the original families still live in many of Ste. Genevieve's old houses. The graceful homes, furnished with fine antiques, are thrown open to visitors during the mid-August *Jour de Fete*. The festival also features crafts, folk dancing, parades, and a grand ball. The town takes pride in the fact that John James Audubon, the famous wildlife painter, lived there for a while in 1811.

From Ste. Genevieve, the road winds north to St. Louis, ending a whirlwind tour of the Show Me State. The memories that crowd the visitor's mind, however, often are more of people than of places. Missourians are courteous, helpful, and proud of their home state. Like their favorite son, Harry Truman, they do their level best and give life all they have.

FACTS AT A GLANCE

GENERAL INFORMATION

Statehood: August 10, 1821, twenty-fourth state

Origin of Name: The correct translation of the name "Missouri" from the Illinois language is probably "people of the big canoe" or "town of the big canoe."

State Capital: Jefferson City, founded 1821

State Nickname: Show Me State

State Flag: Three equilateral horizontal stripes of red, white, and blue surround the state seal, which is set in a circle of twenty-four stars to signify that Missouri was the twenty-fourth state. The seal features two grizzly bears holding a circlet that reads "United we stand, divided we fall." They stand on a scroll inscribed with the state motto. A shield divided in two appears in the center of the seal to symbolize that Missouri is united with, but independent from, the federal government. Twenty-four stars appear at the top of the seal. The flag was adopted officially in 1913.

State Motto: *Salus populi suprema lex esto* (The welfare of the people shall be the supreme law)

State Bird: Bluebird

State Flower: Hawthorn

State Tree: Dogwood

State Stone: Mozarkite

State Mineral: Galena

State Musical Instrument: Fiddle

State Insect: Honeybee

State Song: ''Missouri Waltz,'' words by J. R. Shannon, music by John Valentine Eppel as arranged by Frederick Knight Logan, adopted as the official state song in 1949:

> Hush-a-bye ma baby, slumber time is comin' soon.
> Rest yo head upon my breast, while mommy hums a tune.
> The sandman is calling, where shadows are falling,
> While the soft breezes sigh as in days long gone by.
>
> 'Way down in Missouri where I heard this melody,
> When I was a little child on my mommy's knee.
> The old folks were hummin',
> Their banjos were strummin',
> So sweet and low.
>
> Strum, strum, strum, strum, strum,
> Seems I hear those banjos playing once again,
> Hum, hum, hum, hum, hum,
> That same old plaintive strain.
>
> Hear that mournful melody,
> It just haunts you the whole day long.
> And you wander in dreams,
> Back to Dixie it seems
> When you hear that old song.

POPULATION

Population: 4,916,759, fifteenth among the states (1980 census)

Population Density: 70.5 people per sq. mi. (27.2 people per km²)

Population Distribution: 68.1 percent of the population live in the cities and towns; 31.9 percent live on farms. Nationwide, 73.7 percent of the population live in urban areas.

St. Louis	453,085
Kansas City	448,033
Springfield	113,116
Independence	111,806
St. Joseph	76,691
Columbia	62,061
Florissant	55,372
University City	42,738

(Population figures according to 1980 census)

Population Growth: Missouri's central location as the Gateway to the West was a major factor in the rapid expansion in its population between 1810 and 1900. This

110

increase dwindled after 1900, however, and since then the population growth has not kept pace with the increase in the population of the United States as a whole. Between 1970 and 1980, Missouri's population increased 5.1 percent compared to an 11.45 percent increase nationwide. The list below shows Missouri's population growth since 1810:

Year	Population
1810	19,783
1820	66,586
1840	383,702
1860	1,182,012
1880	2,166,665
1900	3,106,665
1920	3,404,053
1940	3,784,664
1960	4,319,813
1980	4,916,759

GEOGRAPHY

Borders: Eight states share some border area with Missouri: Iowa on the north; Illinois, Kentucky, and Tennessee on the east; Arkansas on the south; and Oklahoma, Kansas, and Nebraska on the west. The Missouri River forms the northwestern border of the state as far south as Kansas City. The Mississippi forms the eastern border, except for the extreme northeastern corner of the state, which is defined by the Des Moines River.

Highest Point: Taum Sauk Mountain in the St. Francois Mountains, south of St. Louis in Iron County, 1,772 ft. (540 m)

Lowest Point: St. Francis River, in Dunklin County, 230 ft. (70 m)

Greatest Distances: North to south—300 mi. (483 km)
East to west—240 mi. (386 km)

Area: 69,697 sq. mi. (180,515 km²)

Rank in Area Among the States: Nineteenth

Rivers: Missouri is crisscrossed by 50,000 mi. (80,465 km) of rivers and streams. The main rivers are the Mississippi and the Missouri. When these two rivers are combined, they account for the majority of navigable river mileage in the United States. Major tributaries of the Mississippi River in Missouri are the Salt River, in the north, and the Meramec, St. Francis, Current, and Black rivers in the south. Tributaries of the Missouri include the Gasconade, Osage, Tarkio, Platte, Grand, and Chariton rivers. These rivers provide drainage for the northern Ozarks, western Ozarks, and the southern plains. Other important rivers in Missouri are the Des Moines; the White River, whose many dams form some of Missouri's largest reservoirs; and the Jacks Fork River. About 86,000 acres (34,803 hectares) along the Current and Jacks Fork rivers are protected as the Ozark National Scenic Riverways.

There are more than ten thousand springs in the Ozarks. Big Spring, in Carter County, is the largest of these springs. Nearly five thousand caves have been found that were formed by underground Ozark springs.

Lakes: Missouri's largest lakes are artificial, the result of the need for hydroelectric energy and for flood control. The largest of Missouri's major reservoirs are Bull Shoals Lake, Clearwater Reservoir, Harry S. Truman Reservoir, Lake of the Ozarks, Pomme de Terre Reservoir, Table Rock Reservoir, and Lake Wappapello. The Lake of the Ozarks on the Osage River is one of the largest man-made lakes in the world and one of Missouri's main tourist attractions. Created by Bagnell Dam, it covers 58,000 acres (23,472 hectares) and has 1,375 mi. (2,213 km) of shoreline. Migrating geese and ducks stop at the national wildlife refuges of Swan Lake, near Brookfield, and Squaw Creek, in Mound City. More than three hundred bald eagles winter in these refuges.

Topography: Much of Missouri's topography is a result of the action of glaciers that covered the northern half of North America in the Ice Age. Two of these glaciers reached as far south as the Central Plains area. The edge of the glaciers melted in the summers, and the runoff formed the Missouri, Mississippi, and Ohio rivers. The Missouri River roughly defines the southwest border of the glaciers. Smaller creeks were also formed by the melted ice. After these creeks dried up, the rich sediment from their banks was carried by the winds and deposited over the Plains area. This loess, or rich silt, is the basis for northern Missouri's agriculture.

Missouri's topography can be divided into four distinct regions: the Glaciated Plain, the Osage Plains, the Ozark Highlands, and the Mississippi Alluvial Plain.

The two open Plains regions are located north and west of the Ozarks. The Glaciated Plains slope gently upward to the north, rising from approximately 650 ft. (198 m) near St. Louis to 1,250 ft. (381 m) in the northwest corner of the state. The Osage Plains, a triangular region, extends below the Missouri River toward the southwest. The prairies are generally flat, but the monotony is broken by streams and low-lying hills as the plains near the Ozarks. The loess deposits provide farmers with deep, evenly textured, fertile soil. When the pioneers first came to the plains, however, the soil was hidden under thick prairie grasses that were nearly 7 ft. (2 m) high.

The Ozark Highlands cover the southern portion of Missouri from southern Illinois through St. Louis and extend west to Oklahoma and south to Arkansas. These are small mountains with average heights of 1,200 to 1,700 ft. (366 to 518 m). Rough hills lie between the Plains and the Highlands.

The Ozark Uplift is the oldest geographical feature in Missouri. These ancient mountains were formed long before the glaciers covered the northern continent. The central crests of the mountains have weathered and are relatively level, but the edges are marked by sharp ridges and deep valleys. Many centuries of leaching and erosion have left the soil in this region much less fertile than that of the prairies to the north.

**Violas and bittersweet
are among the plants
that grow in Missouri.**

The Alluvial Plain in southeast Missouri is a flat area of river plains similar to the Mississippi Delta. The alluvial deposits here are very rich and fertile. This was swampland until the beginning of the twentieth century, but it has been drained and is now a productive agricultural area.

Climate: Weather variations can be sudden in Missouri, but the temperature seldom falls below -10° F. (-23° C) or rises over 100° F. (38° C). The average annual temperature statewide is 55° F. (13° C), with the temperature in January averaging 31° F. (-0.6° C) and the July temperature averaging 77° F. (25° C). Summers and winters are more moderate in the Ozarks than in the northern prairies, which lack the protection afforded by the low-lying mountains.

The highest temperature on record is 118° F. (48° C), recorded in 1936 at Clinton. The lowest temperature, -40° F. (-40° C), was recorded in 1905 at Warsaw.

Rainfall is more frequent in the southeastern portion of the state than in the northern prairies. Average rainfall in the southeast is 47 in. (119 cm), while in the northwest the average is 36 in. (91 cm). The annual precipitation for all of Missouri is 33 in. (84 cm), with the most rain falling in the months of May and June. Some snow also falls in the winter months, averaging 20 in. (51 cm) in the northwest and 6.5 in. (16.5 cm) in the southeast.

NATURE

Trees: Two-thirds of Missouri was covered in virgin timber at the time of settlement. Roughly one-fourth of the state is now forested, primarily in second-growth oak and hickory. Cottonwood, maple, ash, elm, bald cypress, walnut, red cedar, and pine are also common.

Wild Plants: Native plants include violets, anemones, buttercups, wild roses, dandelions, star grass, bluet, phlox, asters, columbines, goldenrod, wild grapes, ivy, honeysuckle, and bittersweet.

Animals: All of the elk, black deer, bison, and antelope found by early settlers are gone. Coyotes, rabbits, opossums, skunks, raccoons, muskrats, red foxes, fox squirrels, rattlesnakes, and copperheads still survive in the less populated areas.

Birds: Native birds include robins, bluebirds, bluejays, woodthrushes, cardinals, blackbirds, orioles, meadowlarks, owls, hawks, crows, quail, wild turkeys, and doves. Canada geese and bald eagles winter in the wildlife refuges.

Fish: Largemouth and smallmouth bass and crappies are found in the Ozark streams and many of the lakes. Trout, catfish, sunfish, carp, walleye pike, perch, buffalo fish, sturgeon, eels, and minnows may also be found in the lakes and reservoirs.

GOVERNMENT

The Missouri state government consists of three branches: legislative, executive, and judicial. The legislative branch, also called the General Assembly, is bicameral. The senate's membership is fixed at 34. The house of representatives has 163 members, but the state constitution allows for this number to change according to population. This apportionment takes place every ten years and is overseen by a separate bipartisan committee. In 1988, Missouri voters authorized regular annual sessions of the General Assembly that run from January through May. Senators serve a four-year term and representatives serve a two-year term. One-half of the members of the General Assembly are elected every two years.

The executive branch has six executive officers: the governor, lieutenant governor, secretary of state, attorney general, treasurer, and auditor. It is limited by a 1972 constitutional amendment to no more than fourteen departments. All officers serve four-year terms and all but the auditor are elected in presidential election years. In 1965, a constitutional amendment allowed the governor and lieutenant governor to serve two terms, which may or may not be consecutive. The governor has line-item veto power over the state budget, and may veto legislation. The governor's veto may be overridden by a two-thirds vote of each house. The governor also appoints judges. The departments under the supervision of the executive branch include the departments of consumer affairs, natural resources, transportation, public safety, social services, agriculture, and education.

In Missouri, the majority of judges are selected through the 1940 "nonpartisan court plan." The state supreme court justices; the judges of the three districts of the court of appeals; the circuit and probate court judges of the city and county of St. Louis, Kansas City, Jackson, Platte, and Clay counties; and the St. Louis court of criminal correction are appointed by the governor. The governor selects the judges from a list of nominations drawn up by a nonpartisan commission. The voters decide on retention of the appointees after they have served one year in office and when their term expires. All other judges are elected by partisan ballots. The supreme court has seven members who serve for twelve years. The three courts of appeals have 31 judges who serve for six years. The 131 judges of the circuit district courts serve for four years.

The voters of Missouri may put measures on a ballot through the initiative and referendum processes.

Number of Counties: 114, plus 1 city—St. Louis— which has the powers of a county

U.S. Representatives: 9

Electoral Votes: 11

Voting Qualifications: Eighteen years of age, registered with the state by the fourth Wednesday prior to any election

EDUCATION

Missouri's public school system was established in 1820 and started operating in 1839. The public schools for elementary and secondary students are administered by local school boards. There are 544 local school districts. The school system is overseen by the state board of education, which appoints a commissioner of education. The commissioner directs the state department of education.

About 800,000 students are enrolled in elementary and secondary public day schools. The student/teacher ratio is about sixteen students to each teacher and per-student expenditure is about $3,000. More than 63 percent of all Missourians over the age of twenty-five have a high school education and nearly 14 percent have completed at least four years of college.

Financing is a primary problem for Missouri's public schools. The state finances about 40 percent of the cost of the schools. The local school boards must finance the remaining 60 percent by submitting a tax levy to the people for a vote. Each new tax levy must be voted on. In most communities, a two-thirds majority is required for approval. Few increases were approved in the 1980s.

About 15 percent of Missouri's students attend private schools. The majority of these private schools are run by the Catholic church. There is no public assistance to parochial schools, though debate has increased over this issue in recent years.

Missouri has ninety-two institutions of higher education, in which about 240,000 students are enrolled. The University of Missouri was founded in 1839 and is the oldest state university west of the Mississippi River. It now has four campuses— Columbia, Rolla, Kansas City, and St. Louis. The journalism school at Columbia campus is the oldest journalism school in the world. The Columbia campus also houses one of the largest college libraries in the United States. Missouri also supports a number of other state universities and colleges: Northwest Missouri State University, at Maryville; Northeast Missouri State University, at Kirksville; Southeast Missouri State University, at Cape Girardeau; Southwest Missouri State University, at Springfield; Missouri Western State College, in St. Joseph; Missouri Southern State College, in Joplin; and Harris-Stowe State College, in St. Louis.

Lincoln University, in Jefferson City, was originally established for recently freed slaves in 1866, but since 1954 has been desegregated. Public junior colleges were authorized in 1962 and they now exist in twelve districts.

Missouri also boasts of two major private universities—St. Louis University, founded in 1818, and Washington University, also in St. Louis, founded in 1853. Many smaller colleges also have excellent reputations, including Cardinal Glennon College and Maryville College, both in St. Louis, and Westminster College, in Fulton. There are a number of smaller denominational colleges, most of which offer professional schooling and seminary training.

ECONOMY AND INDUSTRY

Principal Products:

Agriculture: Soybeans, corn, winter wheat, sorghum grain, hay, fescue seed, feed grain, rice, apples, watermelons, dairy products, beef cattle, dairy cattle, hogs, turkeys, chickens, feeder pigs, breeding hogs, sheep, horses, mules

Manufacturing: Heavy machinery, automobiles, trucks, military and aerospace equipment, processed foods and beverages, medicines, chemicals, electrical equipment, clothing, primary and fabricated metals

Natural Resources: Lead, cobalt, cement, stone, iron ore, coal, barite, clays, lime, zinc, copper, sand, gravel, silver, charcoal, walnut trees, red cedar trees

Business and Trade: Although Missouri is best known for its manufacturing, tourism, and agriculture, it is an important business center as well. More than five hundred thousand Missourians are employed in wholesale and retail trade establishments. Fourteen *Fortune 500* companies and two *Inc. 100* companies have their headquarters in Missouri. Anheuser-Busch, McDonnell Douglas, General Dynamics, and Ralston Purina, among other companies, base their operations in the state. The Kansas City Board of Trade engages in the world's largest hard winter wheat exchange.

Communication: Missouri has more than 250 weekly newspapers and 50 daily papers. The major papers serving the state are the *St. Louis Post-Dispatch*, the *Kansas City Times*, and the *Kansas City Star*. There are about 220 radio stations and 25 television stations in Missouri.

Transportation: Missouri has always served as a transportation hub, as the Missouri and Mississippi rivers were once the main transportation routes in the central United States. Transportation by railroad, barge, highway, and air is still one of Missouri's main businesses. St. Louis and Kansas City are two of the largest and busiest inland ports for barge traffic in the United States, and St. Louis is the busiest port on the Mississippi River. Lambert Airport in St. Louis is the eighth-busiest airport in the United States. Both St. Louis and Kansas City are bases for many major trucking lines and railroads. There are about 8,000 mi. (12,874 km) of railroad track in operation.

The St. Louis Art Museum, in Forest Park

Missouri has more than 9,000 mi. (14,484 km) of federal and primary state highways, including five interstate routes. The state maintains more than 100,000 mi. (160,930 km) of surfaced roadway to link rural and urban areas.

SOCIAL AND CULTURAL LIFE

Museums: Many of the museums in Missouri are related to the state's role in the settlement of the West. A prime example of this is the Museum of Westward Expansion beneath the Gateway Arch in St. Louis. Other St. Louis museums include the St. Louis Art Museum, the National Museum of Transportation, the Old Courthouse, the Missouri Historical Society, the Eugene Field House, Campbell House, and the Museum of Science and Industry. Museums in Kansas City include the Kansas City Museum, the Mormon Visitor's Center, the Nelson Gallery of Art and Mary Atkins Museum of Fine Arts. The Kansas City Art Institute offers an accredited art school. The State Historical Society, in Columbia, showcases a collection of paintings by Missouri artists, as does the capitol in Jefferson City. The Pony Express Museum, in St. Joseph, commemorates the site where the Pony Express began. The Mark Twain Boyhood Home and Museum, in Hannibal, contains more than four hundred exhibits, and the Harry S. Truman Library and Museum, in Independence, showcases memorabilia and papers related to Truman and his presidency.

117

Libraries: More than a hundred Missouri communities maintain libraries. These are financed by local taxes and by some state assistance. The Kansas City Public Library houses about 1.3 million volumes and the St. Louis Public Library houses about 1.5 million volumes. The Missouri State Library helped set up a statewide data base that makes interlibrary loans possible throughout the state. There are also two large history libraries, one operated by the State Historical Society, in Columbia, and the other by the Missouri Historical Society, in St. Louis. The Harry S. Truman Library in Independence is a tourist attraction, as well as a primary source for scholars studying Truman and his presidency. The Linda Hall Library in Kansas City houses one of the most complete collections on science and technology in the Midwest. The largest subscription library in the state is the Mercantile Library in St. Louis.

Performing Arts: The St. Louis Symphony, under the direction of Leonard Slatkin, performs in Powell Hall and is considered one of the top symphonies in the nation. Kansas City supports an excellent regional symphony, and there are many smaller symphonies, such as the Springfield Symphony. The larger cities also support opera and dance companies.

The Starlight Theatre in Kansas City is a popular attraction that offers summer musical performances in the 78,000-seat Swope Park amphitheater. The "Shepherd of the Hills" pageant is produced nightly during the summer months near Branson.

There are numerous annual festivals celebrated throughout Missouri. The National Crafts Festival in Silver Dollar City re-creates life in a mining town. The Maifest, a German festival in Hermann, celebrates the history of the large German-ancestry population living in this area. There is also the V. P. (Veiled Prophet) Fair (a Fourth of July celebration) and the National Ragtime and Classic Jazz Festival, in St. Louis; the American Royal Livestock, Horse Show and Rodeo, in Kansas City; and Tom Sawyer Days, in Hannibal. The Missouri State Fair, in Sedalia, is celebrated annually in the third week of August.

Sports and Recreation: Missouri supports a number of professional sports teams: baseball's American League Kansas City Royals and National League St. Louis Cardinals; football's National Football League Kansas City Chiefs; and the National Hockey League St. Louis Blues.

The varied geography of Missouri offers numerous recreational opportunities. The Ozarks is one of the favorite vacation spots in the United States. The clear streams and large man-made lakes offer excellent fishing, boating, camping, and hunting. White-tailed deer and quail are popular game, and most recreational lakes offer a year-round open season on fish.

National forest areas in Missouri include the Mark Twain National Forest, which covers 1,439,669 acres (582,620 hectares) and features hundreds of miles of streams and hundreds of caves. The fifty-three state parks, forests, and recreation areas include Deer Run, whose 115,105 acres (46,582 hectares) make it the largest of the six state forests. Missouri also operates forty-seven state parks ranging in size from the 65,000-acre (26,305-hectare) Lake of the Ozarks to the 121-acre (49-hectare) Lewis and Clark State Park.

Science and nature attractions also are popular. The Missouri Botanical Garden, in St. Louis, features the Climatron, a geodesic dome that houses a collection of tropical plants. The St. Louis Zoological Gardens are well known for the natural settings in which 2,500 animals are displayed. The Kansas City Zoo also features exotic animals, as does the popular Exotic Animal Paradise at Stafford. There are two planetariums, one at the Kansas City Museum of Science and Industry and one at the St. Louis Science Center.

St. Louis is also a center for convention activity. The Cervantes Convention Center seats more than 16,000 people. The Six Flags Over Mid-America Amusement Park is located 25 mi. (40 km) southwest of St. Louis.

Historic Sites and Landmarks:

Amoureaux House, in Ste. Genevieve, is one of the oldest Creole homes in existence. Built in 1770, it is located on the site of the first permanent settlement in Missouri.

Arrow Rock State Historic Site, near Marshall, is part of an early nineteenth-century town that was located near the meeting of the Santa Fe Trail and the Missouri River. Among the historic buildings that have been preserved are the *George Caleb Bingham House* (1837) and the *Arrow Rock Tavern* (1834).

Bethel German Communal Colony, in Bethel, was founded in 1845 by settlers of German ancestry. More than thirty of the original buildings remain, including a working blacksmith shop.

Bollinger Mill State Historic Site, near Burfordville, displays a turbine-powered grist mill built in 1799. One of the four covered bridges remaining in Missouri is also located here.

First State Capitol State Historic Site, in St. Charles, was the center of government for Missouri from 1821 to 1826.

Fort Davidson State Historic Park, in Ironton, marks the site of a fierce battle between Union and Confederate troops. In twenty minutes of fighting, more than a thousand men were killed or wounded. The Union victory stopped the Confederate drive on St. Louis. Only the earthwork of the fort remains today.

Fort Osage, in Independence, is a restoration of the first United States outpost in the Louisiana Purchase territory. Eighteenth-century furnishings and a museum designed to demonstrate the operation of an Indian trading post may be seen.

Gateway Arch, at the Jefferson Expansion Memorial in St. Louis, is placed over the site of Pierre Laclède's trading post, the first building in what was to become St. Louis. It commemorates St. Louis's role as the Gateway to the West for thousands of pioneers. Designed by Eero Saarinen, it is 630 ft. (192 m) tall. Visitors may ride to an enclosed observation deck at the top of the arch.

Pony Express Stables Museum, in St. Joseph, marks the home of the Pony Express. It is now a museum exhibiting the history of St. Joseph during the eighteen months the Pony Express was in service.

State Capitol, in Jefferson City, is a Roman Renaissance-style building. The original capitol was burned in 1837, as was a second one in 1911. The present structure was built in 1917. It houses a collection of Missouri art, including a Thomas Hart Benton mural depicting Missouri's history.

Trail of Tears State Park, near Cape Girardeau, contains a portion of the route taken by the Cherokees during their forced march from Tennessee to Oklahoma in 1838.

Wilson's Creek National Battlefield, near Springfield, was the site of the first major Civil War battle fought west of the Mississippi. Brigadier General Nathaniel Lyon died in the battle, the first Union general to die during the Civil War.

Other Interesting Places to Visit:

Anheuser-Busch Brewery, in St. Louis, occupies more than seventy city blocks. Visitors may tour the Clydesdale stables, the brewhouse, and the packing plant.

Boone's Lick State Historic Site, near Booneville, preserves the two salt springs (licks) used by Daniel and Nathan Boone (Daniel's sons) to make salt between 1806 and 1814.

Bridal Cave, in Camdenton, is known for its impressive onyx formations and varied, beautiful colors.

Daniel Boone Home, in Defiance, is actually his son Nathan's home and the place in which the famous frontiersman died.

Fantastic Caverns, in Springfield, is one of Missouri's largest caves. During its colorful history, it has served as a speakeasy, a meeting place and, in the 1960s, a country-music theater.

General John J. Pershing Boyhood Home State Historic Site, in Laclede, is a museum devoted to the life of the leader of the American Expeditionary Forces (AEF) during World War I.

George Washington Carver National Monument, near Joplin, preserves the birthplace of the noted black American agricultural chemist and educator. Displays inform the visitor about Carver's life and his work in botany and scientific agriculture.

Harry S. Truman Birthplace State Historic Site, in Lamar, is the restored birthplace of President Truman.

Harry S. Truman Library and Museum, in Independence, houses the papers and memorabilia of the thirty-third president's tenure in office. President Truman's grave is located in the courtyard.

Costumed actors entertain visitors at the Jesse James Birthplace and Museum in Kearney.

Hunter-Dawson State Historic Site, in New Madrid, is the restored home of merchant William Hunter. It is furnished as it would have been in the nineteenth century.

Jesse James Home, in Kearney, marks the place where James was born and where he and his brother Frank grew up.

Jesse James Home, in St. Joseph, was the home of Jesse James and his family after he decided to lead a law-abiding life. He was shot to death here by Robert Ford, a member of his gang. Some original items belonging to the family remain, as does the bullet hole in the wall.

John Wornall House, in Kansas City, is a restored Greek Revival-style plantation house with period furnishings and a formal herb garden.

Laura Ingalls Wilder-Rose Wilder Lane Home and Museum, in Mansfield, is the home in which Wilder wrote her seven *Little House on the Prairie* books. The museum displays memorabilia of both Laura Ingalls Wilder and her daughter Rose, also a noted author.

Liberty Memorial, in Kansas City, honors Kansas City men and women who were killed in World War I. Two museum wings display war relics.

Mark Twain Cave, near Hannibal, appeared in *The Adventures of Tom Sawyer* as the cave in which Tom and Becky Thatcher were lost. This cave is electrically lighted, but nearby *Cameron Cave* has been left in its natural state. Both are open to visitors.

Mark Twain's Boyhood Home and Museum, in Hannibal, was the home of Samuel Clemens from the time he was seven until he was eighteen.

Meramec Caverns, near Stanton, have had a varied history since their discovery in 1716. During the Civil War, they served as storage space for Union forces and an Underground Railroad station. In later years, Jesse James and his band of outlaws used them as a hideout.

Missouri Botanical Garden, in St. Louis, is one of the world's oldest botanical gardens. Its features include a fragrance garden for the visually impaired, a traditional Japanese garden, waterfalls, and the Climatron, a geodesic dome that houses an exceptional collection of tropical and subtropical plants.

Silver Dollar City, near Branson, is a reconstruction of an Ozark mining town. Demonstrations are given of traditional crafts such as pewter spinning, gunsmithing, and log-cabin construction. Many festivals take place annually, including the National Crafts Festival in September.

Swan Lake National Wildlife Refuge, in Brookfield, is one of four national wildlife refuges in Missouri. It is the winter grounds for one of the largest concentrations of Canada geese in North America, and more than one hundred bald eagles winter here.

Thomas Hart Benton Home and Studio State Historic Site, in Kansas City, is a Victorian-style house with a carriage-house studio that was the home of one of Missouri's most famous twentieth-century artists.

USS Inaugural, on the Mississippi River near St. Louis, is a minesweeper that saw service in the World War II Battle of Okinawa.

Winston Churchill Memorial Library, on the Westminster College campus in Fulton, is housed in the Church of St. Mary the Virgin. The church was destroyed during the London blitz. After the war, it was dismantled and brought to Fulton, where it was rebuilt on the campus. The museum contains Churchill letters, paintings, and memorabilia. Westminster College was the site of Churchill's "Iron Curtain" speech in 1946.

IMPORTANT DATES

c. 10,000 B.C.—Bluff Shelter People first inhabit the Missouri area

c. 2000 B.C.—Mound Builders develop a high level of culture in the Mississippi Valley

A.D. 1500s—The first Europeans—Spanish and French—arrive in the region

1673—French explorers Father Jacques Marquette and Louis Jolliet discover the mouth of the Missouri River during their exploration of the Mississippi River

1682—René-Robert Cavelier, Sieur de La Salle, explores the Mississippi River southward to its mouth and claims the Mississippi Valley for France, calling it Louisiana for King Louis XIV

1700—Jesuit priests establish the first mission in Missouri near the site of present-day St. Louis

1720—Philip Renault arrives with black slaves to open a silver mine, but finds only lead

1724—Fort Orleans is established to protect the French settlers and the Indians in the area from Spanish military incursions

1750—The first permanent settlement in Missouri is founded at Ste. Genevieve by Creole settlers from Kaskaskia, Illinois

1762—France cedes the territory of Louisiana west of the Mississippi River to Spain

1763—Through the Treaty of Paris following the French and Indian War, France loses Canada and all possessions east of the Mississippi River to England

1764—St. Louis is founded by Pierre Laclède and René Auguste Chouteau

1800—Napoleon forces Spain to return the western Louisiana Territory to France

1803—The Louisiana Territory is purchased by the United States from Napoleon for $15 million

1804—The formal transfer of the Louisiana Territory is made at St. Louis, giving the United States control of the vital Mississippi waterway; the Lewis and Clark expedition leaves St. Louis

1808—The *Missouri Gazette*, the first Missouri newspaper, is published by Joseph Charless in St. Louis

1809—The St. Louis Missouri Fur Company is organized; Herculaneum is laid out by Moses Austin and soon replaces Ste. Genevieve as Missouri's center for producing lead shot

1811—The first of a series of shattering earthquakes hits New Madrid

1812—The Missouri Territory is organized by the United States Congress; settlement by pioneers begins

1817—The *General Zebulon M. Pike*, the first steamboat to reach the city, arrives at St. Louis

1818—Missouri applies for statehood as a slave state; St. Louis University is founded as the St. Louis Academy

1819 — The steamboat *Independence* proves the Missouri River to be navigable

1820 — Henry Clay's Missouri Compromise is passed by the United States Congress; Missouri is to be admitted as a slave state and Maine as a free state

1821 — Missouri is admitted as the twenty-fourth state in the Union; Kansas City is established as a trading post; the state capital is located at Jefferson City and building starts on the capitol building

1822 — The American Fur Company is started in St. Louis by John Jacob Astor

1831 — Mormon leader Joseph Smith and his followers come from Ohio to found their "New Jerusalem" settlement in Independence

1833 — Mormons are driven from Jackson County

1834 — The *St. Louis Herald*, the first daily newspaper in Missouri, begins publication

1835 — *Anzeiger des Westens*, the first German newspaper in Missouri, is established

1836 — The Platte Purchase, the last treaty made with Native Americans in Missouri, adds six northwest counties to Missouri and ends all Indian claims to the Missouri area

1837 — The capitol building in Jefferson City burns down

1839 — The University of Missouri is chartered at Columbia as the University of the State of Missouri

1841 — The first emigrant wagon trains bound for California leave Independence; the University of Missouri opens its doors to students

1845 — A communal settlement for German immigrants is established at Bethel by Dr. William Keil

1847 — St. Louis is illuminated by gaslight and is connected to the East by telegraph

1849 — The Great St. Louis Fire burns the heart of the city

1852 — The *Missouri Democrat* begins publication; the first railroad track is laid in Missouri between St. Louis and Cheltenham

1853 — Washington University is chartered in St. Louis as the Eliot Seminary; the state's first public high school opens in St. Louis

1857 — The Supreme Court's decision in the Dred Scott case rules that slavery cannot be prohibited in territories of the United States

1858—The first overland mail service stagecoach reaches St. Louis from California; serious violence erupts between Missouri and Kansas over slavery

1859—The first railroad crosses Missouri, connecting Hannibal and St. Joseph

1860—Pony Express service begins in St. Joseph

1861—Missouri votes not to secede from the Union; Union forces win the first battle of the Civil War at Booneville; Union troops under General Nathaniel Lyon are defeated by Confederate troops in the Battle of Wilson's Creek

1865—The Civil War ends; a new state constitution outlaws slavery; it contains an ''Ironclad Oath'' stating that no one who could not swear they had never aided the southern cause could hold office or vote

1866—Lincoln Institute, later Lincoln University, is founded for recently freed slaves

1867—Women are admitted to the normal school at the University of Missouri; an eight-hour-workday law is passed, but not enforced

1869—Hannibal Bridge, the first to span the Missouri River, is built at Kansas City

1872—Edward Campbell Simmons forms the Simmons Hardware Company in St. Louis, the first United States corporation to be engaged in retail sales; women are admitted to all colleges at the University of Missouri

1873—The first public kindergarten is opened in St. Louis

1874—Eads Bridge, the largest steel-arch bridge ever built, opens at St. Louis

1875—A new constitution restores voting rights to Confederate sympathizers; a grasshopper plague devastates crops

1878—Joseph Pulitzer merges two newspapers to form the *St. Louis Post-Dispatch*

1880—The St. Louis *Advocate*, the first black-oriented newspaper in Missouri, begins publication

1881—St. Louis streetcar workers strike

1904—The St. Louis World's Fair commemorates the centennial of the Louisiana Purchase; the first Olympic Games held in the United States take place at the exposition

1908—The University of Missouri establishes the world's first journalism school at its Columbia campus

1911—The capitol building burns again

1917 — The new capitol at Jefferson City is completed

1918 — General John J. Pershing leads American forces fighting in World War I

1921 — Missouri's first radio station, WEW at St. Louis University, goes on the air

1924 — Tom Pendergast and his political machine gain control of Kansas City

1927 — Charles Lindbergh flies nonstop across the Atlantic in the *Spirit of St. Louis*; a tornado in St. Louis kills 87 and injures 1,500

1931 — Bagnell Dam on the Osage River is completed; it supplies hydroelectric power and forms Lake of the Ozarks

1934 — The state sales-tax law goes into effect

1937 — The Missouri legislature creates a program of social assistance for children and the elderly

1944 — General Omar Bradley commands American forces during the World War II invasion of Europe

1945 — Harry S. Truman becomes president

1947 — The first television station in Missouri, KSD-TV in St. Louis, begins broadcasting

1952 — Missouri is declared a disaster area after a serious drought

1955 — Tornadoes in Kansas and Missouri kill 115 people

1957 — The Harry S. Truman Library and Museum is opened in Independence

1959 — St. Louis is declared a disaster area after a series of tornadoes kills 22 people, injures 5,350, leaves 500 homeless, and causes property damage exceeding $12 million

1965 — The Gateway Arch of St. Louis, designed by Eero Saarinen, is topped out

1972 — St. Louis and Kansas City begin extensive urban-renewal projects

1973 — Flooding of the Missouri and Mississippi rivers devastates large areas of Missouri; damage is estimated at more than $100 million

1980 — More than 300 people die in a heat wave; voter approval of a government tax and spending lid helps create a series of financial crises for the state during the 1980s

1981 — Court-ordered school desegregation in St. Louis is carried out peacefully

1982 — Times Beach, a suburb of St. Louis, is abandoned because of a possible spread of dioxin during a flood; serious dioxin contamination has since been confirmed at fifty other sites in Missouri

1984 — Margaret Kelly and Harriett Woods become the first women to hold statewide office in Missouri

1985 — The St. Louis Cardinals and the Kansas City Royals meet in the first all-Missouri World Series; the Royals win

1986 — Economic problems continue to plague the state; workers lose their jobs, businesses fail, and farmers are forced to sell their land; the worst floods in the history of the area hit central Missouri

1988 — A federal judge orders the desegregation of the Kansas City public schools

1989 — The federal education department announces that Missouri is one of only three states to be in compliance with federal civil-rights laws concerning public higher education

1990 — Governor John Ashcroft signs an educational bill that includes a provision allowing parents to choose the public school that their children will attend

IMPORTANT PEOPLE

Zoe Akins (1886-1958), born in Humansville; poet and playwright; received the 1935 Pulitzer Prize in drama for *The Old Maid*

William Henry Ashley (1778?-1838), fur trader, manufacturer, explorer; invented the *rendezvous*, in which the mountain men brought furs to trade for supplies brought to the West by Ashley's company; lieutenant governor of Missouri (1820)

Josephine Baker (1906-1975), born Freda Josephine McDonald in St. Louis; entertainer and jazz singer; starred in Broadway musicals and in Paris revues

Thomas Hart Benton (1782-1858), politician; U.S. senator from Missouri (1821-51); U.S. representative (1853-55)

Thomas Hart Benton (1889-1975), born in Neosho; painter; grandnephew of Senator Benton; his artistic style became known as Regionalism; his murals hang in the state capitol and in the Harry S. Truman Library

Lawrence Peter ''Yogi'' Berra (1925-   ), born in St. Louis; professional baseball player and coach; catcher with the New York Yankees (1946-63); well known for quotes such as ''it's never over 'till it's over''

JOSEPHINE BAKER

THOMAS HART BENTON

"CALAMITY JANE"

ADOLPHUS BUSCH

DALE CARNEGIE

GEORGE W. CARVER

Charles Edward Anderson (Chuck) Berry (1926-   ), born in St. Louis; singer, composer; considered by many to be the "father of rock 'n' roll"; his first record, "Maybelline," was an instant hit; other recordings include "Johnny B. Goode" and "School Days"

George Caleb Bingham (1811-1879), grew up in Franklin and Columbia; painter; his paintings depict pioneer life, river scenes, and political events in the Missouri River Valley

Francis Preston Blair, Jr. (1821-1875), lawyer, politician; helped organize the Free Soil party; U.S. representative from Missouri (1857-64); led the formation of the Republican party in Missouri; was instrumental in keeping Missouri from joining the Confederacy

Susan Elizabeth Blow (1843-1916), born in St. Louis; educator; opened the first public kindergarten in the U.S. in St. Louis (1873)

Omar Nelson Bradley (1893-1981), born in Clark; career U.S. army officer; as a brigadier general, he commanded the U.S. ground troops during the D-Day invasion of France in 1944; General of the Army (1950)

Robert Somers Brookings (1850-1932), merchant, philanthropist; founding president of the corporation of Washington University (1897-1928); was responsible for initiating the upgrading of its medical school; founder of the Washington, D.C., institutions that were later merged to form Brookings Institution

Martha Jane Cannary Burke (1852?-1903), known as "Calamity Jane"; born in Princeton; frontier scout and mail carrier

Adolphus Busch (1839-1913), businessman, philanthropist; president of Anheuser-Busch Brewing Association (1879-1913)

Dale Carnegie (1888-1955), born in Maryville; writer, lecturer; author of best-selling book *How to Win Friends and Influence People*; organized the Dale Carnegie Institute for Effective Speaking and Human Relations

George Washington Carver (1864?-1943), born near Diamond Grove to parents who were slaves; botanist; his experiments in soil management at Tuskegee Institute led him to encourage cotton farmers to plant peanuts and sweet potatoes to replenish their land; developed hundreds of by-products from peanuts, sweet potatoes, and soybeans; awarded the 1923 Spingarn Medal

Joseph Charless (1772-1834), publisher and editor; founded Missouri's first newspaper, the *Missouri Gazette*, in St. Louis (1808)

René Auguste Chouteau (1749-1829), fur trader, pioneer; helped Pierre Laclède found a trading post in the area that became St. Louis; helped organize the St. Louis Missouri Fur Company

James Beauchamp "Champ" Clark (1850-1921), politician; U.S. representative from Missouri (1893-95, 1897-1921); speaker (1911-19); minority leader (1919-21)

Walter Leland Cronkite, Jr. (1916-), born in St. Joseph; journalist and television newscaster

WALTER CRONKITE

Jay Hanna "Dizzy" Dean (1911-1974), professional baseball player; one of baseball's greatest pitchers; pitched for the St. Louis Cardinals (1932-37) and the Chicago Cubs (1938-41); pitched thirty winning games in 1934; elected to the National Baseball Hall of Fame (1953)

Thomas Anthony Dooley (1927-1961), born in St. Louis; physician; worked to bring medical aid to Vietnamese and Laotian villages and founded Medico, an international medical-aid mission

Rose-Philippine Duchesne (1769-1852), Roman Catholic nun; established schools at St. Charles and St. Louis; beatified (1940)

DIZZY DEAN

Charles Eames (1907-1978), born in St. Louis; designer; best known for his design of "Eames chairs" made of contour-molded plywood; had the first one-man furniture exhibit at New York's Museum of Modern Art

Thomas Stearns (T. S.) Eliot (1888-1965), born in St. Louis; poet, critic; his poem *The Waste Land* (1922) helped revolutionize modern poetry; other well-known works include *Murder in the Cathedral* (1935); *Old Possum's Book of Practical Cats* (1939), which was the basis for the musical *Cats*; and *Four Quartets* (1943); received the 1948 Nobel Prize in literature

Eugene Field (1850-1895), born in St. Louis; journalist, poet; probably best known for his nursery rhymes, such as "Wynken, Blynken, and Nod" and "Little Boy Blue"

CHARLES EAMES

Joseph Folk (1869-1923), lawyer, politician; as an attorney in St. Louis, he exposed widespread corruption in that city; as governor (1905-09), he passed many progressive laws

Richard Gephardt (1941-), born in St. Louis; lawyer, politician; U.S. representative (1979-); as chairman of the House Democratic caucus, he helped negotiate a final version of the Gramm-Rudman amendment; House majority leader (1989-)

Joyce Clyde Hall (1891-1982), manufacturer; after coming to Kansas City in 1910, he and a brother opened a wholesale jobbing business in cards that eventually grew into Hallmark Cards, the largest manufacturer of greeting cards in the world

Robert Anson Heinlein (1907-), born in Kansas City; science-fiction author; his books include *Stranger in a Strange Land*, *Red Planet*, and *I Will Fear No Evil*

Langston Hughes (1902-1967), born in Joplin; poet, writer; his first published poem was "The Negro Speaks of Rivers," still one of his best-known works; other works include *The Dream Keeper* and *Fields of Wonder*; awarded the 1960 Spingarn Medal

T. S. ELIOT

JOHN HUSTON

WILLIAM LEAR

MARIANNE MOORE

JAMES CASH PENNEY

John Huston (1906-1988), born in Nevada, Missouri; motion-picture director; his credits include *The Maltese Falcon, Treasure of the Sierra Madre*, and *Night of the Iguana*

Jesse Woodson James (1847-1882), born in Kearney; outlaw; during the Civil War, joined William Quantrill's Confederate guerrilla raiders; after the war, he formed an outlaw gang that robbed banks and trains

Scott Joplin (1868-1917), composer; got his start in Sedalia; was one of the first ragtime musicians trained to read and write music; his most famous piece was ''Maple Leaf Rag,'' published in 1899 by John Stark, owner of a Sedalia music store; there was a revival of interest in rag after his music was used in the hit movie, *The Sting*

Pierre Laclède (1723?-1778), fur trader, pioneer; considered the founder of St. Louis because the flourishing trading post he established near the junction of the Missouri and Mississippi rivers became the site of a settlement that grew into that city

William Powell Lear (1902-1978), born in Hannibal; electronic engineer and manufacturer; founded Lear, Inc. (1939-62); sold it to form Lear Jet Corp. (1962), which manufactured small jet airplanes

Annie Turnbo Malone (1870-1957), businesswoman; manufactured beauty preparations; her business was headquartered in St. Louis from 1902 to 1930; gave generously to the St. Louis YMCA and the St. Louis Colored Orphans Building Fund

James S. McDonnell (1899-1980), aviation pioneer; founded the McDonnell Aircraft Corporation of St. Louis; the company merged with Douglas Aircraft to become McDonnell Douglas (1967); named to the National Aviation Hall of Fame

Marianne Craig Moore (1887-1972), born in Kirkwood; poet; received 1951 Pulitzer Prize in poetry for *Collected Poems*

Howard Nemerov (1920-   ), poet, novelist; resident of St. Louis; received the 1978 Pulitzer Prize in poetry; poet laureate of the U.S. (1988-   )

Thomas J. ''Boss'' Pendergast (1872-1945), born in St. Joseph; politician; his Democratic party machine controlled Jackson County, including Kansas City; convicted of tax evasion (1939)

James Cash Penney (1875-1971), born in Hamilton; merchant; founded the J. C. Penney Company (1904); in 1924, the five-hundredth J. C. Penney store was opened, in Hamilton

John Joseph ''Black Jack'' Pershing (1860-1948), born in Laclede; career U.S. army officer; general who commanded the American Expeditionary Forces (AEF) that fought in Europe during World War I; received the 1931 Pulitzer Prize in history for his autobiography, *My Experiences in the World War*

Joseph Pulitzer (1847-1911), journalist, publisher; combined the *St. Louis Dispatch* and the *Post* to form the *St. Louis Post-Dispatch* (1880); his will endowed the Columbia School of Journalism and established the Pulitzer Prizes in journalism, letters, and music

Nellie Tayloe Ross (1876-1977), born in St. Joseph; politician; became the first woman governor of a state (Wyoming, 1925-27) when she was elected to complete the term of her husband William Bradford Ross, who died in office; director of the U.S. Bureau of the Mint (1933-53)

Dred Scott (1795?-1858), slave who belonged to a Missouri physician; sued for his freedom, basing his suit on the grounds that he had resided in free territory; the U.S. Supreme Court ruled against him

Harlow Shapley (1885-1972), born in Nashville, Missouri; astronomer; was the first to propose that the sun is located in an outer arm of the Milky Way galaxy

Charles Dillon "Casey" Stengel (1890-1975), born in Kansas City; professional baseball player and manager; outfielder for the Brooklyn Dodgers, Philadelphia Pirates, New York Giants, and other teams (1912-31); as manager of the New York Yankees (1948-60), he led the team to ten American League pennants and seven World Series championships; elected to the National Baseball Hall of Fame (1966)

Andrew Taylor (1828-1917), osteopath; originated the theories of osteopathy; founded the first American School of Osteopathy, in Kirksville (1892)

Sara Teasdale (1884-1933), born in St. Louis; poet; her published collections include *Love Songs* and *Strange Victory*

Virgil Thomson (1896-1989), born in Kansas City; composer, music critic; received the 1949 Pulitzer Prize in music for *Louisiana Story*

Harry S. Truman (1884-1972), born in Lamar; thirty-third president of the United States (1945-53); U.S. senator (1935-45); vice-president (1945)

James Milton Turner (1844-1915), born a slave in St. Louis County; became an educator, civic leader, and diplomat; served in the Civil War; when President Lincoln appointed him minister to Liberia, he became the first African American to hold a significant diplomatic post

Mark Twain (1835-1910), pen name of Samuel Langhorne Clemens; born in Florida, Missouri; writer; spent his boyhood in Hannibal; many of his novels are set in Missouri, most notably *The Adventures of Tom Sawyer* and *Adventures of Huckleberry Finn*

Norbert Wiener (1894-1964), born in Columbia; mathematician; his work *Cybernetics* introduced the concept of information control and communication through machines

JOSEPH PULITZER

NELLIE TAYLOE ROSS

HARLOW SHAPLEY

CASEY STENGEL

ROY WILKINS

Laura Ingalls Wilder (1867-1957), writer; wrote her *Little House on the Prairie* books while living in Mansfield

Roy Wilkins (1901-1981), born in St. Louis; civil-rights activist; worked for the NAACP (1934-77), executive director (1965-77); awarded the Spingarn Medal (1964) and the Presidential Medal of Freedom (1969)

Thomas Lanier (Tennessee) Williams (1911-1983), playwright; grew up in St. Louis; two of his best-known plays are *A Streetcar Named Desire*, for which he received the 1948 Pulitzer Prize in drama, and *The Glass Menagerie*

GOVERNORS

Alexander McNair	1820-1824	Lon V. Stephens	1897-1901
Frederick Bates	1824-1825	Alexander M. Dockery	1901-1905
Abraham J. Williams	1825-1826	Joseph W. Folk	1905-1909
John Miller	1826-1832	Herbert S. Hadley	1909-1913
Daniel Dunklin	1832-1836	Elliott W. Major	1913-1917
Lilburn W. Boggs	1836-1840	Frederick D. Gardner	1917-1921
Thomas Reynolds	1840-1844	Arthur M. Hyde	1921-1925
Meredith M. Marmaduke	1844	Sam A. Baker	1925-1929
John C. Edwards	1844-1848	Henry S. Caulfield	1929-1933
Austin A. King	1848-1853	Guy B. Park	1933-1937
Sterling Price	1853-1857	Lloyd C. Stark	1937-1941
Trusten Polk	1857	Forrest C. Donnell	1941-1945
Hancock Lee Jackson	1857	Phil M. Donnelly	1945-1949
Robert M. Stewart	1857-1861	Forrest Smith	1949-1953
Claiborne F. Jackson	1861	Phil M. Donnelly	1953-1957
Hamilton R. Gamble	1861-1864	James T. Blair, Jr.	1957-1961
Willard P. Hall	1864-1865	John M. Dalton	1961-1965
Thomas C. Fletcher	1865-1869	Warren E. Hearnes	1965-1973
Joseph W. McClurg	1869-1871	Christopher S. Bond	1973-1977
B. Gratz Brown	1871-1873	Joseph P. Teasdale	1977-1981
Silas Woodson	1873-1875	Christopher S. Bond	1981-1985
Charles H. Hardin	1875-1877	John Ashcroft	1985-
John S. Phelps	1877-1881		
Thomas T. Crittenden	1881-1885		
John S. Marmaduke	1885-1887		
Albert P. Morehouse	1887-1889		
David R. Francis	1889-1893		
William Joel Stone	1893-1897		

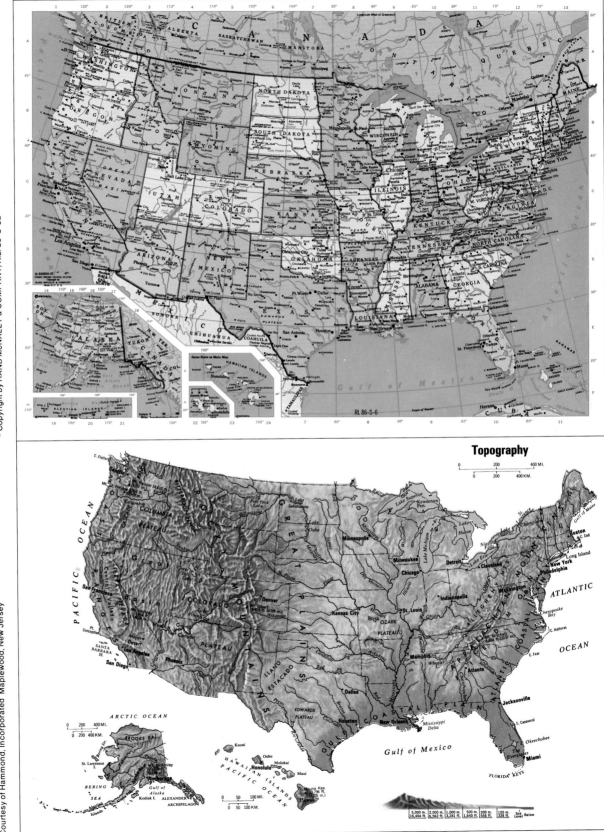

Topography

MAP KEY

Name	Grid
Adrian	C3
Advance	D8
Affton	f13
Albany	A3
Anderson	E3
Appleton City	C5
Arnold	C7
Ash Grove	D4
Ashland	C5
Aurora	E4
Auxvasse	B6
Ava	E5
Bagnell Dam (dam)	C5
Ballwin	f12
Baring	A6
Beaver Creek (creek)	E5
Bel-Nor	f13
Bellefontaine Neighbors	f13
Belton	C6
Berkeley	f13
Bernie	D8
Bethany	A3
Big Creek (creek)	C3
Big Creek (creek)	D5
Big Piney River (river)	D5
Big River (river)	C7
Bismarck	D7
Black Jack	f13
Black River (river)	E7
Bloomfield	D8
Blue Buck Knob (hill)	E5
Blue River (river)	k10
Blue Springs	h11
Bolivar	D4
Bonne Terre	D7
Boonville	C5
Bourbeuse River (river)	C6
Bourbon	C6
Bowling Green	B6
Branson	E4
Braymer	B4
Bread Tray Mountain (mountain)	E4
Breckenridge Hills	f13
Brentwood	f13
Bridgeton	C7
Brookfield	B4
Brunswick	B4
Bryant Creek (creek)	E5
Buckner	h11
Buffalo	D4
Bull Shoals Lake Reservoir (reservoir)	E4
Burke City	E5
Butler	C3
Cabool	D5
California	C5
Calverton Park	f13
Camdenton	D5
Cameron	B3
Campbell	E7
Canton	A6
Cape Girardeau	D8
Cardwell	E7
Carl Junction	D3
Carrollton	B4
Carterville	D3
Carthage	D3

Name	Grid
Caruthersville	E8
Cassville	E4
Castle Point	f13
Castor River (river)	D7
Cedar Creek (creek)	C5
Cedar Hill	C7
Centralia	B5
Chaffee	D8
Chariton River (river)	A5
Chariton River, East Fork (river)	E8
Charleston	B4
Chillicothe	B5
Clarence	B6
Clarence Cannon Lake (lake)	C7
Clark Mountain (mountain)	E5
Clarkton	E8
Clayton	f13
Clearwater Lake Reservoir (reservoir)	C6
Clinton	C4
Cole Camp	C4
Columbia	C5
Concord	f13
Concordia	C4
Crane	E4
Crestwood	f13
Creve Coeur	f13
Crocker	D5
Crowleys Ridge (ridge)	E7
Crystal City	C7
Cuba	f13
Current River (river)	E8
Dardenne Creek (creek)	C7
De Soto	C7
Dellwood	f13
Des Moines River (river)	A6
Des Peres	f13
Dexter	D7
Dixon	E8
Doe Run	D7
Doniphan	E7
Doolittle	D6
Drexel	C3
Duenweg	f13
East Prairie	E8
Edina	B4
El Dorado Springs	D3
Eldon	C5
Eleven Point River (river)	E6
Ellington	D7
Ellisville	f12
Elsberry	B6
Elvins	D7
Eureka	f13
Excelsior Springs	B3
Fair Grove	D4
Fairfax	A2
Farmington	D7
Fayette	B5
Ferguson	C7
Festus	D7
Flat River	D7
Florissant	f13
Forsyth	E4
Fort Leonard Wood (U.S. Army Post)	D6
Fox River (river)	A6
Frankford	B6

Name	Grid
Fredericktown	D7
Fulton	C6
Gainesville	E5
Gallatin	B3
Garden City	C3
Gasconade River (river)	C6
George Washington Carver National Monument	D3
Gerald	C6
Gideon	E8
Gladstone	h10
Glasgow	B5
Glasgow Village	f13
Glendale	f13
Golden City	D3
Goodman	E3
Gower	B3
Grain Valley	E3
Granby	E3
Grand River (river)	A3
Grandview	C3
Grant City	A3
Green City	A5
Greenfield	D3
Greenwood	C3
Hamilton	B4
Hannibal	B6
Hardin	B4
Harrisonville	C3
Harry S. Truman Reservoir (reservoir)	C4
Hayti	E8
Hayti Heights	E8
Hazelwood	f13
Herculaneum	C7
Hermann	C6
Higbee	B5
Higginsville	C4
High Ridge	f12
Hillsboro	C7
Holden	C4
Hollister	E4
Horine	C7
Hornersville	E7
Horse Creek (creek)	D4
Houston	D6
Humansville	D4
Iberia	C5
Illmo	D8
Imperial	C7
Independence	h11
Ironton	D7
Jackson	D8
James River (river)	E4
Jasper	D3
Jefferson City	C5
Jennings	f13
Joplin	D5
Kahoka	A6
Kansas City	C7
Kearney	C6
Kennett	f12
King City	D6
Kinloch	C7
Kirksville	f13
Kirkwood	A6
Knob Noster	D7
La Belle	E8
La Grange	B6
La Monte	D7
La Plata	E7
Ladue	D6
Laddonia	B6
Lake Lotawana (lake)	C3
Lake of the Ozarks (lake)	D5
Lake Taneycomo (lake)	E8
Lake Wappapello Reservoir (reservoir)	A5
Lamar	D3
Lancaster	C5
Lathrop	E6
Lawson	D7
Lead Hill (hill)	f12
Leadwood	B6
Lebanon	D5
Lees Summit	f12
Lemay	B4
Lexington	B3
Liberty	A2
Licking	D6
Lilbourn	B5
Lincoln	C7
Linn	C5
Lockwood	D7
Locust Creek (creek)	f13
Long Mountain (mountain)	E4
Louisiana	D6
Lutesville	A6
Macon	B6

Name	Grid
Malden	E8
Manchester	f12
Mansfield	D5
Maplewood	B5
Marceline	B4
Marionville	D5
Marshall	E8
Marshfield	f13
Marston	A3
Maryland Heights	B3
Maryville	D7
Matthews Mountain (mountain)	B4
Maysville	B3
Medicine Creek (creek)	f13
Mehlville	A5
Memphis	C7
Meramec River (river)	D6
Meramec River, Dry Fork (river)	B6
Mexico	A4
Milan	C7
Miner	B4
Mississippi River (river)	B5
Missouri River (river)	E4
Moberly	B6
Monett	C6
Monroe City	E8
Montgomery City	D8
Morehouse	A2
Morley	E8
Mound City	f13
Mount Vernon	D5
Mountain Grove	D6
Mountain View	g13
Murphy	D3
Nevada	C6
New Florence	B5
New Franklin	C6
New Haven	B6
New London	E4
New Madrid	D6
Newburg	D5
Niangua River (river)	A2
Nixa	E3
Nodaway River (river)	C7
Noel	A3
Norborne	D7
Normandy	E8
North Fabius River (river)	D6
North Kansas City	D4
Northwoods	D5
O'Fallon	h11
Oakville	C6
Odessa	C4
Olivette	D5
Oran	C5
Oregon	B5
Orrick	B2
Osage Beach	B3
Osage Fork (river)	C5
Osage River (river)	D5
Osceola	C3
Overland	C4
Owensville	A2
Ozark	D7
Ozark Plateau (highlands)	E6
Pacific	A4
Palmyra	D6
Paris	E5
Parkville	C5
Parma	A4
Peculiar	C7
Perry	B5
Perryville	B3
Pevely	E8
Piedmont	C3
Pierce City	A4
Pine Lawn	C7
Pinnacle, The (hill)	C7
Platte City	l12
Platte River (river)	E6
Plattsburg	D6
Pleasant Hill	D6
Pleasant Valley	B6
Point Lookout	D6
Pomme de Terre Lake Reservoir (reservoir)	C4
Pomme de Terre River (river)	C4
Poplar Bluff	C4
Portage Des Sioux	C4
Portageville	B4
Potosi	D5
Pottawatomie River (river)	D3
Princeton	f13
Purdy	B4
Puxico	B6
Queen City	C7

Name	Grid
Raymore	C3
Raytown	h11
Republic	D4
Rich Hill	C3
Richland	D5
Richmond	B4
Richmond Heights	f13
Rock Hill	f13
Rock Port	A2
Rogersville	D4
Rolla	D6
Sac River (river)	D4
Salem	D6
Salisbury	B5
Salt River (river)	B5
Salt River, Middle Fork (river)	A5
Salt River, North Fork (river)	B6
Salt River, South Fork (river)	f13
Sappington	D3
Sarcoxie	B3
Savannah	D8
Scott City	C4
Sedalia	E7
Seneca	E3
Senath	D5
Seymour	f13
Shelbina	E8
Shelbyville	E8
Sikeston	B4
Silex	B3
Slater	B3
Smithville	A5
Smithville Lake Reservoir (reservoir)	C3
South Fabius River (river)	l13
South Grand River (river)	D3
Spanish Lake	D4
Spring River (river)	C7
Springfield	C6
St. Ann	E7
St. Charles	D7
St. Clair	D6
St. Francis River (river)	l13
St. Francois Mountains (mountains)	B3
St. James	D4
St. Johns	C7
St. Joseph	A3
St. Louis	D7
St. Peters	D6
Ste. Genevieve	E8
Steele	B3
Steelville	D4
Stewartsville	D4
Stockton	C5
Stockton Lake Reservoir (reservoir)	D4
Stover	B5
Strafford	h11
Sturgeon	C6
Sullivan	C4
Sweet Springs	D5
Table Rock Lake (lake)	C3
Tarkio	E4
Taum Sauk Mountain (mountain)	A2
Thayer	D7
Thompson River (river)	E6
Thorny Mountain (mountain)	A4
Timbered Knob (hill)	D6
Tipton	E5
Trenton	C5
Troy	A4
Union	C7
Unionville	B5
University City	B3
Valley Park	E8
Van Buren	C3
Vandalia	A4
Versailles	C7
Viburnum	C7
Warrensburg	l12
Warrenton	E6
Warsaw	D6
Washington	D6
Waverly	B6
Waynesville	D6
Webb City	C4
Webster Groves	C4
Wedgewood	C4
Wellington	C4
Wellsville	B4
Wentzville	D5
West Fork Cuivre River (river)	D3
West Plains	f13
Weston	B4
Wheaton	B6
Whiteman Air Force Base	C7
Willard	B6

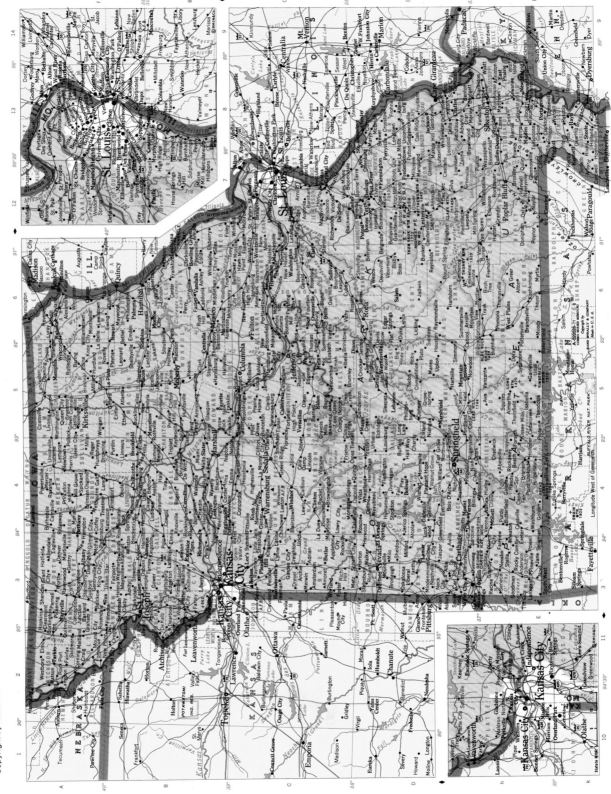

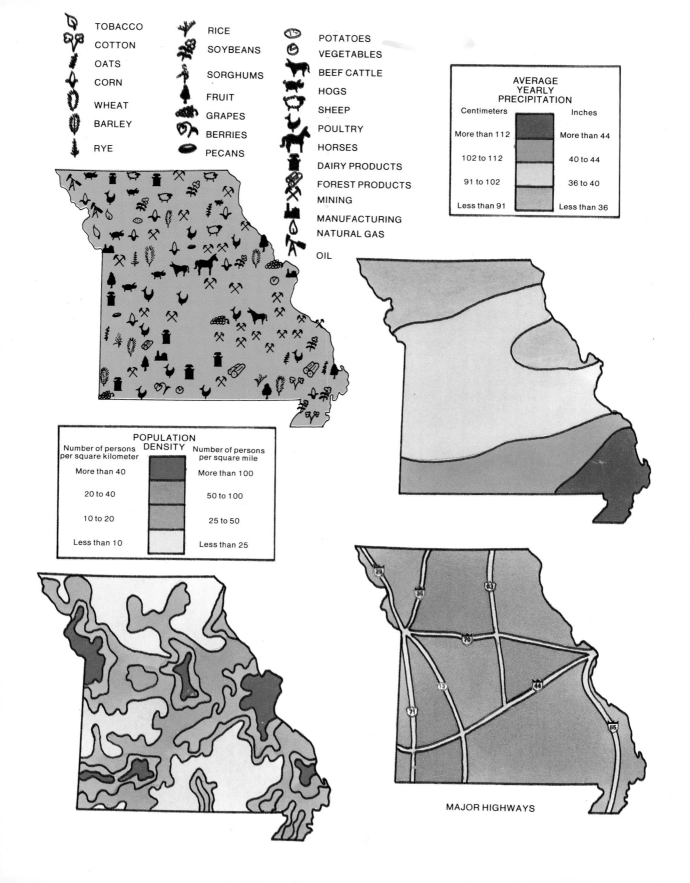

TOBACCO
COTTON
OATS
CORN
WHEAT
BARLEY
RYE

RICE
SOYBEANS
SORGHUMS
FRUIT
GRAPES
BERRIES
PECANS

POTATOES
VEGETABLES
BEEF CATTLE
HOGS
SHEEP
POULTRY
HORSES
DAIRY PRODUCTS
FOREST PRODUCTS
MINING
MANUFACTURING
NATURAL GAS
OIL

AVERAGE
YEARLY
PRECIPITATION

Centimeters		Inches
More than 112		More than 44
102 to 112		40 to 44
91 to 102		36 to 40
Less than 91		Less than 36

POPULATION
DENSITY

Number of persons per square kilometer		Number of persons per square mile
More than 40		More than 100
20 to 40		50 to 100
10 to 20		25 to 50
Less than 10		Less than 25

MAJOR HIGHWAYS

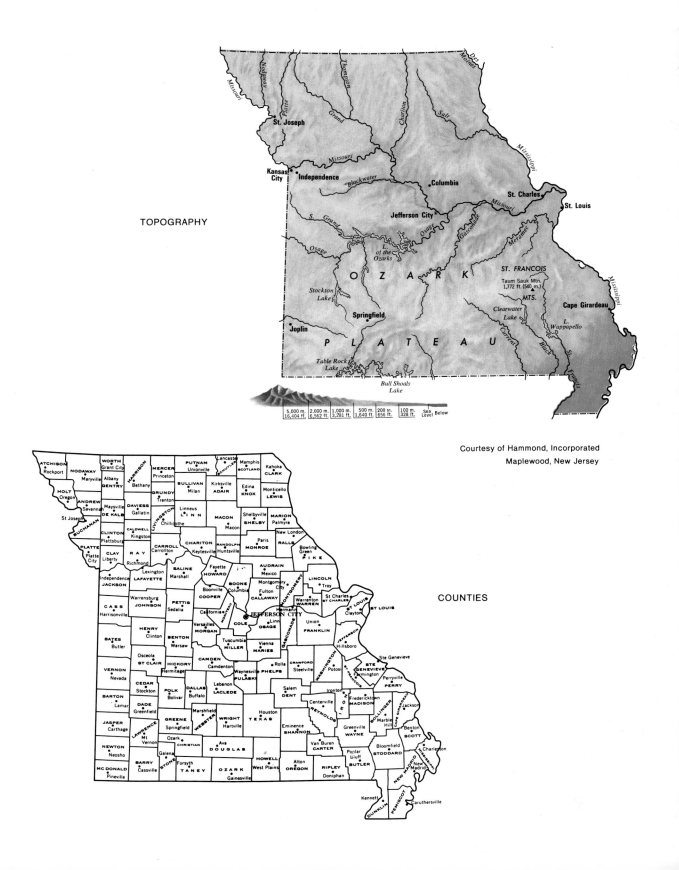

TOPOGRAPHY

COUNTIES

Missouri farmland

INDEX

Page numbers that appear in boldface type indicate illustrations

1.2 billion-year-old rocks are a feature of Elephant Rocks State Park, in Iron County.

Picture Identifications

Front cover: St. Louis at dusk
Back cover: Alley Spring Mill, Jacks Fork, Ozark National Scenic Riverways
Pages 2-3: Lake Springfield at sunset
Page 6: The Gateway Arch and the Old Courthouse
Pages 8-9: A Missouri River Valley farm, near Dutzlow
Pages 20-21: A montage of Missourians
Pages 26-27: *Pierre Laclède Landing at the Present Site of St. Louis*
Pages 40-41: *Raftsmen Playing Cards*, an 1847 oil painting by George Caleb Bingham
Pages 54-55: Festival Hall and the Cascades, with boats on the Grand Lagoon at the 1904 St. Louis World's Fair
Page 68: The Missouri State Capitol at Jefferson City
Pages 78-79: The *Mark Twain* cruises the Mississippi below Hannibal
Pages 92-93: A view of downtown St. Louis from across the river
Page 108: Montage showing the state flag, state tree (dogwood), state bird (bluebird), and the state musical instrument (fiddle)

About the Authors

William Sanford and Carl Green have written more than seventy books for children and young adults. Dr. Sanford grew up in New Haven, Connecticut and went on to earn degrees at Wesleyan University (B.A.), the University of Texas (M.A.), and the University of Southern California (Ph.D.). Dr. Green is a native Californian whose degrees are from the University of California Santa Barbara (B.A.), California State University Long Beach (M.A.), and the University of Southern California (Ph.D.). The authors each taught high school social studies for more than thirty years before retiring to spend more time on their writing. Both are seasoned travelers who live with their wives in the South Bay area of Southern California. Roxanne Ford, who compiled the Facts at a Glance section, is a graduate of Pomona College. She works as a records administrator for a private foundation in Los Angeles.

Picture Acknowledgments